D1333239

013839854 4

Asian dishes are often high in salt and so the recipes in this book have been adapted to contain substantially less than traditional versions. Most of the recipes contain low to moderate levels of fat, saturated fat and sugar. Readers who wish to reduce the salt levels further could consider using lower-salt soy and stock.

1 3 5 7 9 10 8 6 4 2

Published in 2013 by Ebury Press, an imprint of Ebury Publishing

A Random House Group Company

Text © Gok Wan 2013

Inside food photographs: © Romas Foord 2013

Inside author photographs: © Mark Read 2013

Cover author photographs: © Trevor Leighton 2013

Gok Wan has asserted his right to be identified as the author of this Work in accordance with the Copyright, Designs and Patents Act 1988

All rights reserved. No part of this publication may be reproduced, stored in a retrieval system, or transmitted in any form or by any means, electronic, mechanical, photocopying, recording or otherwise, without the prior permission of the copyright owner.

The Random House Group Limited Reg. No. 954009

Addresses for companies within the Random House Group can be found at www.randomhouse.co.uk

A CIP catalogue record for this book is available from the British Library

The Random House Group Limited supports the Forest Stewardship Council® (FSC®), the leading international forest-certification organisation. Our books carrying the FSC label are printed on FSC®-certified paper. FSC is the only forest-certification scheme supported by the leading environmental organisations, including Greenpeace. Our paper procurement policy can be found at www.randomhouse.co.uk/environment

To buy books by your favourite authors and register for offers visit www.randomhouse.co.uk

FSC MIX Paper from responsible sources FSC® C004592

Project editor: Laura Herring

Design: Two Associates

Inside photography: Romas Foord (food) and Mark Read (author)

Cover photography: Trevor Leighton

Food stylist: Robert Allison

Stylist: Sam Duffy

Dietician: Fiona Hinton

Chinese revolutionary girl (p34) Chinese noblewoman (page 203) and tree peony (front cover and page 224) © Getty
Portrait of Wu Die on page 103 © Corbis

Colour origination by Altaimage, London

Printed and bound by Firmengruppe APPL, aprinta druck, Wemding, Germany

ISBN 978 0 0919 5703 2

G

OK'S

WOK

EBURY
PRESS

CONTENTS

I love Asia. I love the people; I love the climate; I love the shopping. But it is the food that really blows me away every time. Asian cooking has a simplicity of flavour and a freshness of ingredients that you won't find in any other cuisine on Earth. And, if I'm being completely honest, it appeals to my inner showman. Asian food looks far more complicated than it is, and when I serve it up in the middle of my dinner table it always creates a bit of theatre and drama. Its vivid clash of colours literally makes me beam with joy!

I think Asian food is in a league of its own because of how it is constructed — there is a perfect balance of sweet caressing sour, contrasting with salt, while holding its own against spicy. Like a perfectly put together outfit, each element works in harmony, enhancing all your best bits so it can make a bold, confident entrance.

Part of my love of Asia and Asian cooking also comes from my guilt of not knowing very much about it until I was in my twenties. When I was growing up, I hated being half Chinese. I hated being different and I was bullied and picked on; everything about Asia felt a bit bad. But around the dinner table my Dad would tell us stories about his homeland and I began to learn about my Chinese heritage through the food we shared together. It wasn't until I first visited Thailand on holiday when I was 25 that my true obsession with Asia began. Before I knew it, I was leaping on to planes to Hong Kong and Singapore, discovering all the wonderful colours and flavours Asia had to offer. And every time I visit one of these amazing and inspiring countries, the souvenirs I am looking for are the recipes I can take home, to remind me of the wonderful people and places I have seen.

Food is at the core of every Asian family and life begins and ends at the dinner table. Every occasion – whether it's a wedding or a funeral – centres around a massive sharing table where you're given your foundation of rice and then you choose your meat, fish and veggie dishes to go with it. You often share anywhere between 8 and 20 dishes around the table, with your chopsticks touching those next to you, almost as though you're holding hands. But sharing a meal doesn't need to be an elaborate feast of lobster, suckling pig and duck; it can be as simple as a bowl of broth. I think taking the time to sit down and eat a meal together is one of the most basic principles of living, and cooking for your loved ones lets them know how much you appreciate them. Learning to share a meal is the biggest gift I've ever been given and now I want to pass it on to you.

BUT I get it . . . you're busy: three kids in the bath, a partner late home from work and a washing machine full of wet clothes. How many of us have the time to cook quick and healthy recipes from scratch? The simple answer is: all of us!

It's not that I'm being a total smartarse. Well, actually, I am. It's just that I sometimes feel like I don't have enough hours in my day either! I'm a self-confessed workaholic, speeding through my life at 100 miles per hour, adjusting bra straps and hoiking up hemlines as I go. But to sustain this lifestyle, I need a diet that fuels me, fascinates me . . . occasionally flirts with me, but above all, satisfies me. And I'm confident that you want all this, too. Well, fear not, my little culinary cuties, this book is stuffed with delicious recipes that do just that.

As some of you may know, when I was 21, I lost a staggering 10 stone of weight. Up until that point I overindulged on an average of 74 takeaways a day! And, as

much as I loved eating that kind of food, I soon realized that it wasn't a healthy lifestyle choice. Overnight, I dropped a lifetime of fatty foods, and, although it wasn't done in a healthy way, it wasn't until that point that I learned that what I ate was directly responsible for how I felt. It was then that I began to teach myself the art of healthier cooking and almost instantly I knew what I had to do: adapt the recipes I loved to create healthy, satisfying, flavoursome Asian-fusion foods.

Since becoming an adult Wan, I have taken many of the recipes my family have taught me and carefully edited them to fit my lifestyle. Within one working week I can be in three different cities, two countries and on several shoots. Whether I'm shooting a fashion, food, dating or game show, you can be guaranteed that the one thing I will try to do is eat well: I know that if I don't eat right there is no way I will have the energy to complete my busy schedule.

Even though we never had lots of money when we were growing up, we always ate like kings or, in my case, a 'queen'. And that's what my father has taught me: in life, you only need good food and family. So how do you eat well without spending a fortune and without compromising on flavour? The rules are simple: moderation, balance and fresh ingredients. For me, convenience food isn't about dried packets and ready-made meals, it's what it says on the tin: about making food convenient. I work hard and I need my food to work even harder. So this book is full of tasty, balanced recipes that are packed to the hilt with flavour and made from ingredients that will keep you living to the age of 104 (although we can't guarantee that, of course!).

The main concerns of people who don't have a wok or who aren't familiar with Asian food are the time it will take to prepare, the complexity of the ingredients, and the insecurity that they may fail. I promise you that if you allow me to show you how, you will not fail – it's not even an option! These recipes are all about adding to your repertoire, and, once you have learned a few key skills and are familiar with the basic ideas, you can make them your own.

Along the way, my recipes will take you on a culinary journey to the four corners of Asia. We will dip our toes into the warm seas of South-East Asia, climb the mountains in China, jump ship to Korea before ending up in Singapore where we will bathe in every other cuisine this amazing continent has to offer.

My Chinese heritage has had an incredibly important impact on my life, but being raised Anglo-Asian has led me to appreciate both of my cultures. This book is filled with recipes that are very much fusion dishes combining all of my life experiences, whether in a street market in Bangkok or sitting in the English countryside. Because of this you will find many of the ingredients, recipes and techniques are already familiar to you; I've just given them an Asian twist.

As well as fueling us, our food is a silent language we use to communicate with each other and ourselves; it's a powerful tool for telling someone how we feel about them and it's a wonderful vehicle for taking a friend or loved one on a personal journey. Once you have mastered this skill, and learned the gift of giving good food, I guarantee the most satisfying feeling of self-fulfilment. My career has required me to create outfits for every occasion, whether you're working, dating or lounging, and, in my heart, I believe food is the same. Understanding what to eat, when and for what occasion, is as important as living itself, and is an art form that is as skilful as creating the dish itself. I promise you that in this book you will find recipes for the perfect dinner a deux, lunchtime dishes to stop you from falling into the dreaded three o'clock food-slump, and meals that will satisfy but never overload you. The recipes that I've developed for you are healthy, uncomplicated and great to share with your loved ones – or selfishly enjoy in your pyjamas on your own.

❀ I know you have worried about what to wear on a date, but have you ever thought about what to serve on a date?

❀ Have you ever felt like you've been run over by a bus simply because of what you ate for lunch? Has six o'clock ever felt so far away?

❀ If you fantasize about feeling better about your body, these dishes will get you eating your way to confidence in no time.

Kowkhyn's
Room

G LAU CHINESE RESTAURANT

KENYA
UGANDA
TANGANYIKA

1 2 3

Dear Cook,

So here it is: my brand new book stuffed with exciting, healthy and delicious recipes.

I have absolutely loved developing these recipes for you. I hope you have lots of fun making them and I really hope you and your loved ones enjoy every last mouthful.

There are dishes in this book to cater for every part of your life. From healthy lunchtime solutions to tasty, sharing curry feasts. There are ideas for perfect 'date nights', dinner parties and even one-pot wonders you must NEVER share with anyone.

Take what you wish from these recipes and develop them to suit your personal tastes and lifestyle. Think of this book as a best friend's guide to Asian fusion food.

Poppa Wan always says, 'There are two types of people: people who live to eat and people who eat to live.' I know which one I am . . . do you?

All my wokking LOVE,

'If I had to choose between taste or shoes, I would be walking barefoot for the rest of my life.'

QUICK &
HEALTHY

I once ate a bowl of noodles so quickly I sneezed an entire string. I knew from that moment that I had to start eating healthier.

I am a firm believer that we should never be prisoners of our own food war; after all, food is such a wonderful enjoyment, why deny yourself such pleasure? Having said that, I know all of us could be a little healthier . . . think of it as balance! It's not about WEIGHT-LOSS; it's about cleansing.

This chapter is packed full of delicious health-conscious recipes that will help shape your life and leave you feeling contently full and satisfied.

Rice cakes and cottage cheese are all well and good, but, if you're like me, then sometimes your hunger demands a lunch or dinner with bigger balls! There is no point in still being hungry after you've eaten, otherwise you will be a slave to snacking — so, I suggest filling up on tasty healthy foods!

BROCCOLI AND SESAME SOUP

241 CALORIES
16.5g FAT
4.1g SAT FAT
3.2g SUGAR
2.4g SALT

I consider my culinary tastes to be quite honest and rustic, however there is a side of my personality that plays to the flamboyant. I love fine dining, but it's not just about ironed tablecloths and *hot* waiters. It's also about carefully choreographed dishes served with precision. But who has the time or patience? This dish screams fine dining but without the hassle or expense. It is hugely dependent on the natural colours of the ingredients: the deepest of greens juxtaposed with the dark speckles of sesame seeds, contrasted with the poached egg. It is worthy of any cover of *Vogue* – fashion week in a bowl!

SERVES 4

4 eggs

1 large head of broccoli, florets and stalk separated

1 tbsp rice bran oil or vegetable oil

4 spring onions, trimmed and roughly chopped into 2cm pieces

a 2cm piece of fresh ginger, peeled and finely chopped

1L hot, light, low-salt vegetable stock

75g leftover cooked rice (or a packet of instant rice)

a pinch of sugar

2 tbsp soy sauce

1 tbsp sesame oil, plus a little extra to serve

2 fresh red chillies, deseeded and finely chopped

1 tsp black sesame seeds

optional: salt and white pepper

Poach the eggs for 3–4 minutes in gently simmering water, until the white is opaque and the yolk is just firm to the touch. Place in a bowl of cold water until needed.

Chop the stalks of the broccoli into rough 1cm pieces. Heat the oil in a large saucepan over a medium heat. Once hot, add the spring onions, the chopped broccoli stalk and the ginger. Sweat in the hot oil for 1 minute before adding the hot stock, cooked rice and the broccoli florets.

Increase the heat and bring to the boil. Add the sugar and simmer for about 15 minutes, or until everything is very tender and falls apart when pushed lightly with a spoon.

Stir in the soy sauce and sesame oil, and then, using a jug or stick blender, blitz until you have a smooth soup. Taste and season with a little salt and pepper if you think it needs it.

Place a poached egg in the bottom of each soup bowl and pour the soup around the egg. Scatter over the chopped chilli and sesame seeds and drizzle with a little extra sesame oil.

384
CALORIES

22.4g
FAT

4.6g
SAT FAT

6.2g
SUGAR

2.9g
SALT

SALMON TOM YUM

On one of my first ever holidays to Thailand I discovered three things: free foot massages could probably bring world peace, I'm way too tall to buy Thai clothing, and tom yum soup is one of the easiest and most delicious dishes to cook. After a ridiculously busy day on set I crave a wholesome, light meal, so, as soon as I get home, I kick off my shoes, whack on a pan of water to boil and tip in all the ingredients for a tom yum soup. By the time I am in my pyjamas, my meal is ready. Happiness in a bowl.

SERVES 2

600ml hot, light, low-salt vegetable stock (or use a good-quality stock cube)

2 fresh red chillies, split lengthways but still attached at the top

300g salmon fillets, skin removed, cut into 2cm chunks

100g baby spinach leaves

1 carrot, peeled and cut into long slivers using a vegetable peeler

100g bean sprouts

juice of 2 limes

1 tbsp fish sauce

2 tbsp roughly chopped peanuts

Pour the hot stock into a large saucepan (or bring a pan of water to the boil and stir in the stock cube). Add the chillies and bring to the boil over a medium heat. Reduce to a low simmer and add the salmon. Let the salmon poach gently in the stock for 2–3 minutes, until just cooked through.

Place a large handful of spinach leaves in the bottom of each serving bowl and top with the carrot.

Drop the bean sprouts into the hot stock and season with lime juice and the fish sauce. Place the fish on top of the spinach and carrots and pour over the stock and bean sprouts, picking out the chillies. Top with the crunchy peanuts.

488
CALORIES
30.5g
FAT
6.2g
SAT FAT
1.9g
SUGAR
2g
SALT

STEAMED MACKEREL WITH PAK CHOY

Asia is brilliant for convenience cooking. Asian supermarkets are full of packets of wonderful stuff that are quick to prepare but with maximum flavour, making cooking almost effortless. I think everyone should visit a Chinese supermarket a couple of times a year to fill up their store. If you can't get hold of dashi, you can use a light miso soup, and you can also replace the mackerel with any meat or fish – just make sure it's cooked properly.

SERVES 2

2 x 175g fresh mackerel fillets

a 1cm piece of fresh ginger, peeled and finely chopped

2 spring onions, trimmed and finely chopped

1 tbsp soy sauce

1 tsp rice bran oil or vegetable oil

2 heads of pak choy, leaves separated

200ml warm dashi stock or light miso

100g steamed brown rice, to serve

Place the mackerel fillets in a shallow bowl and cover with the chopped ginger, spring onions and soy sauce. Mix well, making sure that everything is worked into the flesh of the fish. Leave to rest at room temperature for a couple of minutes.

Heat the oil in a wok over a high heat. Once hot, add the pak choy and stir-fry for about a minute, just until the leaves begin to wilt. Place the wilted leaves in the bottom of a shallow heatproof dish that will fit inside a steamer basket. Top the leaves with the mackerel fillets, scraping over all of the marinade mixture. Wipe out the wok with some kitchen roll, pour in enough water to come about halfway up the sides and bring to the boil.

Pour over enough dashi or miso to almost cover the pak choy. Carefully lower the dish into your largest steamer basket, and place over the wok of boiling water (making sure the bottom of the steamer doesn't touch the water). Steam for about 8 minutes or until the fish is cooked through. Keep an eye on the water and top up if it starts to dry out.

To feel fully virtuous, serve the mackerel and pak choy with a bowl full of steaming brown rice on the side.

244
CALORIES
10.2g
FAT
3.5g
SAT FAT
1.8g
SUGAR
2.7g
SALT

PORK AND WATERCRESS SOUP

If you want to make this into a more substantial meal then spoon some cooked rice or noodles into the bottom of your bowl before pouring over the soup and meat.

SERVES 4

a 2cm piece of fresh ginger, peeled and finely diced

1 tbsp light soy sauce

600g pork tenderloin, trimmed and sliced into 1cm strips

1 tbsp rice bran oil or vegetable oil

1L hot, low-salt vegetable or chicken stock

1 tbsp oyster sauce

1 tbsp dark soy sauce

4 spring onions, trimmed and finely sliced

150g watercress

white pepper

Place the ginger and the light soy sauce in a shallow dish along with a little pepper. Add the strips of pork and mix well so that the ingredients are well combined and the meat is thoroughly coated. Leave for 5 minutes so that the flavour of the ginger and the soy work into the meat a little.

Heat the oil in a wok over a high heat. Once hot, add the marinated pork and stir-fry for 2–3 minutes until the meat has taken on some colour. It is not necessary to cook the pork all the way through at this point. Once it has browned, transfer to a plate.

Pour the hot stock into the wok and bring to a simmer over a medium to high heat. Pour in the oyster sauce and dark soy sauce, and stir to combine. Carefully drop in the pork, and let it simmer for about 30 seconds to ensure it is fully cooked through.

Ladle your delicious broth into bowls before scattering with the spring onions and finishing with a mound of crunchy watercress.

313
CALORIES

8.4g
FAT

1.9g
SAT FAT

3.3g
SUGAR

1.6g
SALT

EGG NOT-SO FRIED RICE

This is an incredibly easy dish: it's just rice, eggs, soy sauce and a splash of sesame oil, and it's dry-fried, which keeps it healthier than the classic version. The trick is to keep on stirring it and watch it like a hawk so it doesn't start sticking – really go mad with it and move it all around. You can use up any leftover veggies here or throw in a few prawns for a fancier take on a store-cupboard classic.

SERVES 4

2 cloves of garlic, peeled and finely chopped

a 3cm piece of fresh ginger, peeled and finely chopped

4 spring onions, trimmed and finely sliced

1 carrot, peeled and chopped into 1cm dice

75g green beans, trimmed and chopped into 1cm pieces

100g frozen peas

2 eggs

1 tbsp sesame oil

1½ tbsp light soy sauce

600g cooked white rice

2 tbsp shaosing or dry sherry

2 tsp fish sauce

Heat a wok over a medium to high heat. Once hot, add the garlic, ginger, spring onions, carrot and beans. Stirring almost constantly, dry-fry the vegetables for 1 minute. Stir in the frozen peas. While your vegetables are cooking, whisk together the eggs with half of the sesame oil and 1 tablespoon of the soy sauce.

Give your vegetables a good stir and pour in about 3 tablespoons of water. Add the whisked egg mixture. At this point you have to watch the mixture like a hawk and stir as soon as you see the egg beginning to set. The stirring should break up the egg into very small pieces.

Just as it is all beginning to stick to the pan, add your cooked rice to the mix and stir well to combine. The rice should work as an abrasive and pick up anything that has stuck to the base of the wok, but add a splash of water if you think it needs it. Pour in the shaosing, fish sauce and the remaining sesame oil and soy sauce. Mix well, scraping the bottom of the wok.

Serve your much healthier, not-so fried rice to amazed friends and family.

637
CALORIES
39.6g
FAT
8g
SAT FAT
5g
SUGAR
2.4g
SALT

OMEGA-3 DETOX SALAD

This dish is one of my failsafe quick dinners. Mackerel is a super versatile fish that can be eaten hot or cold, and it works particularly well in this recipe with all the Asian seasoning to create a uniquely oriental flavour. It is naturally high in good oils from the fish and perfectly balanced with the fresh herbs and crunchy pomegranate seeds.

SERVES 2

40g shelled unsalted pistachio nuts

3 tbsp roughly chopped fresh mint leaves

3 tbsp roughly chopped fresh coriander leaves

a 1cm piece of fresh ginger, peeled and roughly chopped

1 clove of garlic, peeled and chopped

¼ tsp ground coriander

¼ tsp ground cinnamon

¼ tsp ground cardamom

1 heaped tbsp fat-free Greek yoghurt

1 fresh red chilli, deseeded and roughly chopped

juice of ½ a lime

½ tbsp fish sauce

250g cooked and cooled brown rice

180g smoked mackerel fillets, skin removed, flaked

4 tbsp pomegranate seeds

Place all of the ingredients apart from the rice, mackerel and pomegranate seeds in a small food processor and blend to form a smooth dressing. If necessary, add a little warm water to loosen the mixture.

Pour the dressing over the cooled rice and mix well to coat. Gently fold through the flaked mackerel, pile on to serving plates and finish with a scattering of pomegranate seeds.

514
CALORIES

10g
FAT

2.1g
SAT FAT

8.6g
SUGAR

0.56g
SALT

BROWN RICE TREASURE HUNT

Ginger is a natural remedy for so many ailments, but the only problem is that trying to eat raw chunks of ginger is like trying to eat raw fire. So, if you want an injection of gingery goodness, then look no further than this recipe. The sweetness of the sugar balances the heat of ginger and all sits in perfect harmony with the nutritionally rich brown rice. Prepare this and it won't just be your tummy that thanks you, but your taste buds too.

SERVES 2

a 4cm piece of fresh ginger, peeled and grated

1 tbsp rice wine vinegar

1 tbsp palm sugar or agave nectar

1 tsp sesame oil

350g cooked brown rice, cooled

3 spring onions, trimmed and finely sliced

200g skinless cooked chicken breast, sliced into strips

100g shelled edamame beans

3 breakfast radishes, washed, trimmed and roughly chopped

80g pea shoots

salt

optional: edible flowers

Place the grated ginger in a small piece of muslin cloth. Gather the cloth around the ginger and squeeze the ginger juice into a bowl. Add the vinegar, sugar and sesame oil. Season with a little salt and mix until all the ingredients are well blended together.

Place the cooked rice, spring onions, chicken strips, edamame beans and radishes in a bowl. Pour over the dressing and use a spoon or your hands to lightly mix the salad together.

Pile up the salad on to two plates, garnish with a mound of pea shoots, scatter with edible flowers, if using, and get stuck in.

38
CALORIES
1.1g
FAT
0.4g
SAT FAT
1g
SUGAR
1.1g
SALT

CABBAGE-WRAPPED PORK DUMPLINGS

Who would have thought that cabbage could be so versatile and delicious? These tasty morsels make a great alternative to regular flour dumplings. They are also perfect packed into your lunch box and eaten cold the next day.

MAKES 12

300g lean pork mince

1 tbsp light soy sauce, plus 3 tbsp to serve

a 2cm piece of fresh ginger, peeled and grated

1 clove of garlic, peeled and finely chopped

1 spring onion, trimmed and finely sliced

2 tbsp chopped fresh chives

1 large Chinese cabbage, leaves separated

salt and white pepper

Place the pork, soy sauce, ginger, garlic, spring onion and chives in a bowl and season with salt and pepper. Mix well to combine all of the ingredients.

Take 12 of the best cabbage leaves and trim off the majority of the hard white stalk. (These can be saved and used in stir-fries.)

Place a heaped tablespoon of the pork mixture in the middle of a trimmed leaf. Draw the edges of the leaf together over the meat to create a rough ball. Repeat the process with the remaining mixture and cabbage leaves.

When ready to cook, bring a large saucepan of water to the boil. Place the cabbage parcels in a large steamer basket and place the basket over the boiling water (make sure the bottom of the basket doesn't touch the water). Steam for about 12 minutes, until firm to the touch and fully cooked through. Keep an eye on the water and top up if necessary. Serve, dipped in soy sauce.

308
CALORIES

7.7g
FAT

1.5g
SAT FAT

2.7g
SUGAR

1.6g
SALT

10-MINUTE CHICKEN STIR-FRY

You don't have to use the veggies I've suggested in this simple stir-fry; pretty much anything will work, including cucumber, celery, mange tout and carrots – my Dad sometimes even uses cold Brussels sprouts. It's actually a great way to use up the leftovers from your Sunday roast. Come Monday, after your first day back at work, you can turn those scraps into a quick and delicious evening meal.

SERVES 4

2 tbsp rice bran oil or vegetable oil

300g skinless chicken breast, sliced into 1cm strips

4 cloves of garlic, peeled and roughly chopped

a 3cm piece of fresh ginger, peeled and finely chopped

6 spring onions, trimmed, chopped in half and bashed

80g frozen peas

80g shelled edamame beans

400g cooked and cooled jasmine rice

2 tbsp shaosing or dry sherry

1½ tbsp light soy sauce

1 tbsp dark soy sauce

lemon wedges, to serve

Heat half the oil in a wok over a high heat. Once hot, add the chicken strips and stir-fry for 3 minutes. The chicken should be almost cooked through, but it doesn't need to be fully cooked at this point. Transfer the chicken to a plate and set aside.

Wipe your wok clean with some kitchen roll. Add the remaining oil and heat over a medium to high heat. Add the garlic, ginger and spring onions and stir-fry for 2 minutes. Tip in the frozen peas and edamame beans and stir-fry for a further minute.

Return the chicken to the wok and mix to combine, then stir in the cooked rice. Pour in the shaosing and let it bubble and almost evaporate before pouring in the soy sauces and mixing until everything is well coated.

Serve your quick and healthy chicken stir-fry with wedges of lemon to squeeze over the top.

443
CALORIES
16.3g
FAT
2.7g
SAT FAT
9.2g
SUGAR
3.3g
SALT

SUNRISE NOODLES

Oh, come on . . . be honest! It's late, work has been more than taxing and all you can think about is vegging out on the sofa with a glass of wine. But your hunger is attacking you like a Selfridges' shoe sale! What to do? The same as everyone else: either order in a stomach-stomping pizza or, worse still, ram the entire contents of your fridge into your mouth, not-so-innocently turning a blind eye to whether the food needs reheating or not!

Don't worry; I'm not as guilt free as I may sound. I, too, have been slave to my hunger. But, I have a failsafe, go-to delicious dish that takes literally no time to cook and is super-healthy and filling: Sunrise Noodles. A steaming bowl of clear broth, layered with udon noodles, pak choy, Chinese cabbage and egg, laced with a provocative amount of ginger, garlic and chilli, which will hug you in all the right places until it's time to collapse feeling virtuous and loved.

SERVES 2

1 egg
650ml dashi stock or light miso
2 cloves of garlic, peeled and finely chopped
a 1cm piece of fresh ginger, peeled and finely chopped
1 fresh red chilli, deseeded and finely chopped
1 head of Chinese cabbage, finely shredded
1 head of pak choy, leaves separated
½ tbsp fish sauce
1 tbsp soy sauce
300g straight-to-wok udon noodles, rinsed in boiling water
40g peanuts, roughly chopped

Boil the egg in a saucepan of water for 3–4 minutes, for soft boiled. Once cooked, remove from the heat and cool under running water. Set aside.

Bring the dashi or miso to the boil in a large saucepan over a medium heat. Add the garlic, ginger and chilli and let the broth simmer for 2 minutes.

Add the cabbage, pak choy, fish sauce and soy sauce, and continue to simmer for a further 2–3 minutes, until the leaves are just tender.

Divide the blanched noodles between two large serving bowls. Top the noodles with half of a peeled egg, ladle over the hot broth and scatter with the peanuts. Breathe in the delicious aromas of your satisfying and fulfilling bowl of goodness.

344
CALORIES

21.1g
FAT

5.4g
SAT FAT

5.2g
SUGAR

1.9g
SALT

POPPA WAN'S FU YUNG

This dish isn't necessarily what you'd class as Asian, but my Dad taught me how to make it and I have yellow skin and slanty eyes, so, by default, this dish is very Asian. Essentially, this dish is a 'crab stick' omelette, but it is the dash of sesame oil and the spring onions that give it a nod to the East. You don't have to use seafood sticks, you can use whatever you have available – chicken, prawns or strips of lean beef will all work well.

SERVES 1

2 eggs
1 tsp soy sauce
a few drops of sesame oil
½ tbsp rice bran oil
½ onion, peeled and finely chopped
2 seafood sticks, unwrapped and
    chopped in half
75g frozen peas
white pepper
10g pea shoots, to serve
optional: 1 tbsp chilli sauce, to serve

Crack the eggs into a small bowl and add the soy sauce, sesame oil and a generous pinch of white pepper. Whisk with a fork until all the ingredients are well combined. Keep to one side.

Heat the oil in a wok or small frying pan over a high heat. Once hot, add the onion and stir-fry for 2 minutes, until just beginning to soften. Add the crab stick pieces and frozen peas and continue to stir-fry for a further minute.

Pour in the seasoned egg mixture. Let the egg set a little, before gently stirring. You are aiming for something a little like a scrambled omelette, with large pieces of browned egg mixed with the seafood sticks and peas. Stir-fry all the ingredients together for about 2–3 minutes, until the egg is cooked through.

Slide the egg mixture on to a plate and top with pea shoots. Serve with chilli sauce for a fresh and fiery contrast.

640
CALORIES
36.9g
FAT
9.6g
SAT FAT
2.5g
SUGAR
1.1g
SALT

'PRAWN TOASTS'

When I was growing up, most Saturday afternoons would find my entire family huddled around the long stainless steel preparation bench in the restaurant kitchen, spreading slice after slice of white bread with a mashed prawn paste. We were preparing the prawn toast for the following week's trade. Mum would be at one end of the bench and Dad at the other with the three of us children sandwiched in-between. I loved those days – the whole family together. Although we were working, we were as one, almost a modern-day Waltons family. Who would have thought a tasty piece of fishy bread could be so satisfying both inside and out? This is my version of prawn toasts, which is healthier, but made with just as much love as the one I cooked with my family.

SERVES 4

300g salmon fillets, skin removed

10 large raw king prawns

1 x quantity of flatbread dough (see page 198)

flour, to dust

2 tbsp sesame oil

2 heaped tbsp extra-light cream cheese

2 heaped tbsp crème fraîche

6 tbsp finely chopped fresh dill

2 tbsp finely chopped fresh parsley

4 tbsp finely chopped fresh chives

½ clove of garlic, peeled and grated

1 tbsp fish sauce

2 avocados, stone removed, peeled and chopped into 1cm dice

optional: salt and white pepper

Preheat the oven to 200°C/400°F/Gas mark 6. Bring a saucepan of water to the boil and poach the fish for 3–4 minutes. Add the prawns and simmer for 4 minutes, until the salmon and prawns are just cooked through. Transfer to a plate and leave to cool to room temperature.

Divide the flatbread dough into 4 evenly sized balls. Lightly dust a clean work surface with a little flour and roll each ball into a rough circle about 0.5cm thick. Heat a quarter of a tablespoon of oil in a small frying pan over a medium heat. Cook one of the dough circles for 1–2 minutes, until browned in places and slightly puffed up. Flip over and cook on the other side for a further 2 minutes, until cooked through. Transfer to a plate while you cook the rest of the flatbreads. Leave to cool while you make the filling.

Spoon the cream cheese and crème fraîche into a bowl. Add the chopped herbs, grated garlic, fish sauce and the rest of the sesame oil. Use a spoon to beat the ingredients together until well incorporated.

Gently break the salmon into chunks and roughly chop the cooked prawns. Add the fish and prawns along with the chopped avocado to the creamy mixture. Using an exaggerated stirring action gently fold the fish and avocado through the dressing. Season, to taste, with a little salt and pepper. Spread each flatbread with some of the salmon and prawn mixture. Roll up, slice and serve.

 TIP: To get perfectly round slices, wrap your filled and rolled pancakes in cling film and twist at both ends to seal, like a Christmas cracker. Slice straight through the cling film. These can be made the night before you want to serve them and kept chilled; they will firm up in the fridge.

ASIAN SALADS

I have three main bugbears in the world: dishonesty, mobile phones clipped to belts and, most importantly, the bad rap Asian food gets for being unhealthy.

Asian cuisine is super-healthy due to the incredibly diverse availability of fresh vegetables as a result of the climate and the cooking methods used. For many years, Asian families have boiled, steamed and stir-fried their food.

For all of my Gokettes out there who refuse to compromise on taste but want their jeans to feel a little more comfortable, this chapter is going to accessorize your life like a perfect Chanel handbag. These Asian-inspired salads are virtually guilt free but are packed with so much flavour you would never know you were eating your way to confidence.

There's something hugely self-righteous about tucking into a bowl of fresh crunchy vegetables that have been flirted with the perfect balance of seasoning, lightly dressed, and then adorned with either fish or meat or another protein of your choice.

539
CALORIES
17.7g
FAT
5.2g
SAT FAT
5.9g
SUGAR
1.6g
SALT

BO TAI CHANH BEEF

This is my take on a classic Vietnamese salad. It is a fantastic combination of sweet and sour, crunchy and unctuous. I've used red wine vinegar instead of traditional lime juice to give it a gentle warmth and richness.

SERVES 2

300g trimmed sirloin steak

1 tbsp rice bran oil or vegetable oil

2 tbsp red wine vinegar

2 tsp light soy sauce

1 tsp sugar

a 1cm piece of fresh ginger, peeled and grated

1 clove of garlic, peeled and finely grated

½ red onion, peeled and finely sliced

10g fresh coriander

10g fresh basil

3 tbsp chopped raw peanuts

salt and white pepper

300g cooked brown rice, to serve

Season the steak with salt and pepper. Heat the oil in a wok over a very high heat. Once hot, add the steak and fry for 3 minutes on each side. Transfer to a plate and leave to rest while you prepare the rest of the dish.

Mix together the vinegar, soy sauce, sugar, ginger and garlic until well combined. Add the sliced onion and leave to sit for 2 minutes.

Slice your well-rested steak and top with the onion dressing, the coriander and basil leaves, and scatter over the peanuts.

Serve alongside cooked brown rice for a sumptuous, filling and healthy supper.

332
CALORIES

11.7g
FAT

1.4g
SAT FAT

9.5g
SUGAR

2.2g
SALT

LEMON POACHED CHICKEN

Light, fresh and summery, this salad is a perfectly balanced combination of flavours and textures. There is a lot going on here, but everything is in such harmony that none of the ingredients dominates or overpowers the dish. It's a beautiful bowl and proves that salads definitely do not need be merely an accompaniment to the main event.

SERVES 4

3 stalks of lemon grass

15g fresh coriander, stalks and leaves separated

25g fresh basil, stalks and leaves separated

15g fresh mint, stalks and leaves separated

2 tsp coriander seeds

4 x 125g skinless chicken breasts

5 tbsp lime juice

1½ tbsp palm sugar or agave nectar

2 tbsp fish sauce

1 fresh red chilli, deseeded and finely diced

200g bean sprouts

2 carrots, peeled and chopped into matchsticks

½ a cucumber, peeled, halved lengthways and deseeded, chopped into 1cm slices

100g prawn crackers, to serve

Use a rolling pin to bash two stalks of lemon grass all the way along their length to help release their flavour. Place them in a large saucepan of water along with all of the stalks from the herbs and the coriander seeds. Bring to the boil and then reduce the heat. Add the chicken and simmer – don't boil – for 6 minutes. Turn off the heat and leave to cool for about 30 minutes, by which time the chicken should be fully cooked through.

In the meantime, trim the top and the bottom from the remaining stalk of lemon grass and chop it is as finely as you can. Put the chopped lemon grass in a bowl along with the lime juice, sugar, fish sauce and the chilli. Mix together until well combined and the sugar has dissolved.

Toss together the herb leaves with the bean sprouts, carrot and cucumber. Drizzle over the dressing and mix well to coat.

Remove the chicken from its poaching liquid and, using either your fingers or two forks, shred it into bite-sized pieces. Arrange the chicken on a large serving plate and scatter over the salad.

Serve your deliciously refreshing salad with the crunchy prawn crackers.

211
CALORIES
11.1g
FAT
2g
SAT FAT
15.4g
SUGAR
1.6g
SALT

TOMATO TOM SAM

Classic tom sam is made with fermented fish and green papaya. However, you're unlikely to find these down your local supermarket, so this is my version. I've used tomatoes to make the dressing, bolstered by anchovy fillets, and green papaya is replaced with mooli, which has an irresistibly fresh flavour. Don't let my recipe restrict you, though; this is such a versatile dressing that you'll soon be finding any excuse to make it.

SERVES 2

1 tomato, roughly chopped

1 bird's eye chilli, roughly chopped (seeds removed if you don't like it too hot)

2 tinned anchovy fillets, drained and roughly chopped

2 tsp fish sauce

6 tsp lime juice

2 tsp palm sugar or agave nectar

300g mooli, peeled and finely sliced into matchsticks

1 carrot, peeled and finely sliced into matchsticks

100g bean sprouts

½ cucumber, peeled, halved lengthways and deseeded, finely sliced into matchsticks

2 tsp fresh mint leaves

2 tsp fresh coriander leaves

35g raw peanuts, roughly chopped

2 tsp toasted sesame seeds

Place the tomato, chilli, anchovies, fish sauce, lime juice and sugar in a pestle and mortar. Bash and grind until you have a pulpy consistency that is reasonably smooth. Taste and adjust the seasoning with a little extra lime juice, fish sauce or sugar if you feel it needs it.

Place all the vegetables and herbs in a bowl and pour over the dressing. Mix lightly with your hands before dividing the salad between serving plates and garnishing with the chopped peanuts and toasted sesame seeds.

365
CALORIES
12.3g
FAT
2.8g
SAT FAT
6g
SUGAR
2g
SALT

CHICKEN, CUCUMBER AND BEAN SPROUTS

This dish is one of the reasons why I love cooking. Every now and again you need a dish on your dining table that is elegant, pure and blissfully hassle-free. The flavours are subtle and complement each other perfectly; none of them upstages each other and the dish is beautiful with everything on the same muted colour palette. Sometimes less is most definitely more.

SERVES 2

1 tbsp rice bran oil or vegetable oil

4 spring onions, trimmed and chopped into 2cm pieces

a 1cm piece of fresh ginger, peeled and finely chopped

4 tinned anchovy fillets, drained and roughly chopped

100g green beans, trimmed

½ a cucumber, peeled, halved lengthways and deseeded, chopped into 1cm slices on an angle

4 water chestnuts, roughly sliced

250g bean sprouts

2 tbsp shaosing or dry sherry

1 tbsp oyster sauce

300g cooked chicken, shredded (leftovers are perfect)

white pepper

Heat the oil in a wok over a medium to high heat. When hot, add the spring onions, ginger and anchovies. Stir-fry for 1 minute before adding the green beans, cucumber, water chestnuts and bean sprouts. Continue to stir-fry for a further 2 minutes.

Pour over the shaosing and let it bubble and reduce for a few seconds before adding the oyster sauce and a generous amount of white pepper.

Add the shredded chicken and stir gently to mix and coat in the sauce. Serve as soon as the chicken is hot all the way through.

416
CALORIES

3.7g
FAT

0.6g
SAT FAT

9.3g
SUGAR

2.3g
SALT

SWEET MISO SOBA NOODLES

This salad is so delicious that it's hard to believe it's also good for you. Miso gives the dressing a touch of luxury and its unique and satisfying flavour spreads through all the other ingredients.

SERVES 2

200g soba noodles

1 tsp sesame oil

200ml miso stock

3 spring onions, trimmed and finely sliced

a 1cm piece of fresh ginger, peeled and finely diced

1 clove of garlic, peeled and finely diced

1 tbsp agave nectar or honey

5 water chestnuts, roughly chopped

¼ of a red pepper, deseeded and finely sliced

1 carrot, peeled and finely sliced into matchsticks

25g baby spinach leaves

1 tsp toasted sesame seeds

Cook the noodles according to the packet instructions. Leave to cool and then dress with the sesame oil.

Place the miso in a saucepan and add one of the sliced spring onions, the ginger and garlic. Bring to the boil and then leave to simmer until it has reduced by two-thirds. Remove from the heat.

While still warm, add the agave nectar and stir until dissolved.

Pour the warm miso over the cooked noodles. Add the water chestnuts, red pepper, carrot, the remaining spring onion and the spinach. Mix well before sprinkling with the toasted sesame seeds.

598
CALORIES
1.8g
FAT
0.5g
SAT FAT
12.5g
SUGAR
2.3g
SALT

PRAWN, PAPAYA AND TOMATO

When you think of salad I bet the first thing that comes to mind is soggy lettuce, curled-up cucumber slices and tasteless tomatoes. How could that possibly be tempting and why would anyone in their right mind waste one of their precious three meals a day on that? Well, my little salad dodgers, get your taste buds buckled up because this dish is not only super-delicious, it's also virtually guilt free.

SERVES 2

1 tomato, roughly chopped into 2cm chunks

1 papaya, peeled and roughly chopped into 2cm chunks

1 fresh red chilli, deseeded and finely chopped

½ a red onion, peeled and finely chopped

50g green beans, chopped into 1cm pieces

170g cooked king prawns, shelled

250g vermicelli noodles, soaked and cooled

3 tbsp fresh mint leaves

3 tbsp fresh coriander leaves

FOR THE DRESSING

2 tsp fish sauce

1 stalk of lemon grass, trimmed and very finely chopped

juice of 1 lime

a few drops of sesame oil

1 tsp agave nectar, palm sugar or dark brown sugar

First, make the dressing by mixing together all the ingredients until the agave has dissolved. Leave to one side while you make the salad.

Simply place all of the salad ingredients in a bowl and mix together with your hands. Pour over the dressing and mix again to coat.

Pile on to serving plates, close your eyes and be transported to a warmer climate with every mouthful.

244
CALORIES
9.5g
FAT
1.9g
SAT FAT
7.1g
SUGAR
1.7g
SALT

WARM HOISIN SQUID WITH TENDERSTEM BROCCOLI AND PICKLED CHILLI

Hoisin sauce should be the eighth Wonder of the World. Rich in flavour, texture and depth, just a small amount can transform the most simple of salads. It is commonly coupled with duck, but it's hugely versatile because of its unique flavour. I particularly like it with squid, but don't overdo it, as squid has a far more delicate flavour than duck.

SERVES 2

4 baby squid, cleaned

300g Tenderstem broccoli

1 tbsp rice bran oil or vegetable oil

1 tbsp hoisin sauce

FOR THE PICKLED CHILLI

1 tbsp rice wine vinegar

1 tsp sugar

½ tsp salt

2 fresh red chillies, deseeded and finely sliced diagonally

Start by making the pickled chilli. Mix the vinegar, sugar and salt in a bowl until the sugar and salt have completely dissolved. Add the sliced chilli and leave for a minimum of 5 minutes, but no longer than 30 minutes.

Bring a medium saucepan of salted water to the boil. Separate the tentacles from the main body of the squid and set aside. Slice the squid tubes in half lengthways, so that you now have 8 long pieces of squid. Take one piece and score it on the diagonal at 0.5cm intervals (be careful not to slice the flesh all the way through; although don't worry if you do – it all tastes the same!). Now score it in the opposite direction to create a criss-crossed pattern. Repeat with the remaining squid tubes.

Once the water is boiling, drop in the broccoli and simmer for 2 minutes. Use a slotted spoon to transfer the cooked broccoli to a colander and cool under cold running water.

Bring the water in the saucepan back up to the boil, and drop in the squid, tentacles and all. Cook for 1 minute, then remove and cool under cold running water.

Heat the oil in a wok over a high heat. Once hot, add the well-drained broccoli and stir-fry for 30 seconds before reducing the heat to medium and adding the hoisin sauce and 50ml of water. Stir together and warm through for about a minute or so.

Divide your dressed broccoli between serving plates, top with the poached squid and a little pickled chilli for a fiery finish.

SEAFOOD SALAD WITH GRAPEFRUIT VINAIGRETTE

A salad so luxurious it's hard to believe it's also supremely healthy. The grapefruit gives it a flash of unexpected flavour, but don't worry about it being too bitter, as the sugar offsets any sharpness. This is a salad that is as enjoyable to look at as it is to eat.

SERVES 2

1 ripe pink grapefruit

2 tbsp rice wine vinegar

1 tbsp palm sugar or agave nectar

2 tsp fish sauce

240g cooked and cooled seafood (any combination of prawns, squid, mussels, salmon, lobster and crab sticks)

50g baby spinach leaves

50g pea shoots

75g Chinese cabbage, shredded

40g raw peanuts, roughly chopped

6 rice cakes, roughly broken into large chunks

Peel and segment the grapefruit using a sharp knife. Reserve all the juices and pour them into a small bowl. Set aside the grapefruit pieces.

Add the vinegar, sugar and fish sauce to the grapefruit juice and whisk well until the sugar has dissolved.

Place the grapefruit segments and the cooked seafood in a bowl and add the spinach, pea shoots and shredded cabbage. Spoon over a few tablespoons of the dressing and gently mix the salad with your hands.

Pile up two plates with the salad, spoon over more of the dressing, and then top with the peanuts and rice cake pieces.

441
CALORIES

14g
FAT

2.8g
SAT FAT

17.2g
SUGAR

2.1g
SALT

THREE-BEAN AND SWEET CHILLI SALAD WITH TUNA

This recipe is going to prove just how simple it is to make Asian fusion dishes. Asian fusion is all about taking hints from the East and combining them with very familiar ingredients from the West. Sometimes, a dash of sesame oil, a sprig of fresh coriander or a small slurp of soy is all you need to create an Asian-inspired meal. What I love about this dish is its ease. A few handfuls of different-shaped beans, tossed with a light Asian dressing and served with a grilled tuna steak couldn't be simpler; it is a true testament to the versatility of Asian food.

SERVES 2

2 tbsp sugar

4 tbsp red wine vinegar

2 tsp fish sauce

1 tsp dried chilli flakes (more if you like it hotter)

2 tinned anchovy fillets, drained and very finely chopped

400g mixed beans (a mixture of edamame, peas and broad beans), cooked and cooled

2 spring onions, trimmed and finely sliced

1 clove of garlic, peeled and finely diced

juice of 1 lime

1 tbsp rice bran oil or vegetable oil

2 x 120g tuna steaks

salt and white pepper

Place the sugar in a wok and heat over a medium to high heat for about 3 minutes; it will begin to melt and caramelize. Keep an eye on it, as once it starts melting, it will change very quickly. Once it has turned a lovely rich brown colour, remove the wok from the heat and very carefully pour in the vinegar and fish sauce. Take care, as the mixture will spit. Return the wok to the heat and stir until well combined. Now add the dried chilli flakes. Remove from the heat and set to one side.

Place the anchovy fillets, mixed beans, spring onions and garlic in a bowl and toss together with the lime juice. Pour over the chilli dressing and mix so that the beans are lightly coated.

Wipe out the wok with some kitchen roll, then heat the oil over a medium to high heat. Season your tuna steaks with a little salt and a generous amount of pepper and, once the oil is hot, sear them for 1 minute on each side, or longer if you prefer your tuna cooked all the way through. Serve the tuna with the bean salad.

LUNCHTIME

3 o'clock slump . . . ring any bells? Maybe you had one too many glasses of red the night before or maybe you didn't sleep too well? Whatever the reason, you need to make sure you look after yourself, and what you eat at lunchtime can help aid your recovery.

The average person in the UK works 40+ hours each week, so why not treat yourself to some 'you time' on your lunch break? Take a moment to think alone and enjoy a pot of tasty food that you've prepared yourself, for yourself. It's not being selfish; think of it as taste empowerment. Food should enhance your life and that hour at midday is vital for recharging your mind, body and soul.

It's time to PACK IT UP! One of the most versatile carbohydrates is the noodle. Noodles are used throughout Asian cuisine, so it doesn't matter where you are in this amazing continent, you'll come across a regional noodle dish, whether it's udon in Japan, egg noodles in China, or vermicelli in Thailand. The reason why they are so versatile for lunch, is that they reheat really well, and they are lighter – and generally have fewer calories – than rice.

Or, why not bring the principles of Asian eating to your office and introduce a Thursday lunch club where you each bring in a dish to share around the table? The pack-up revolution has begun. Viva la Tupperware!

PACKED LUNCH BROTH

Either drink this soothing stock on its own to brighten up any time of day, or take it to work in a flask for lunch and pour it over a selection of finely sliced veggies or cooked meat or prawns. Thinly sliced carrots and baby spinach work particularly well with shredded cooked chicken. Just make sure you don't take anything too chunky, as it won't warm through in the broth.

MAKES ABOUT 1.25 LITRES
(250ml/serving)

1.25L miso stock

½ tbsp oyster sauce

1 tbsp fish sauce

1 tbsp light soy sauce

1 spring onion, trimmed and bashed

2 sticks of celery, roughly chopped

1 clove of garlic, peeled and squashed

a 4cm piece of fresh ginger, peeled
    and roughly chopped

white pepper

Place all the ingredients in a large saucepan and season with a generous pinch of pepper. Bring the ingredients to the boil over a medium heat and then reduce the heat and simmer for 15 minutes.

Strain the stock through a fine sieve, discarding all of the vegetables.

 TIP: The stock will keep in the fridge for 3–4 days or you can freeze it for up to 3 months. (Freeze it in portions so you always have some on standby. Simply heat it gently in a saucepan to defrost.)

325
CALORIES
11.5g
FAT
2g
SAT FAT
8.4g
SUGAR
1.7g
SALT

CHICKEN, PEA AND OKRA £2 CURRY

If you were to calculate how much you spend on your shop-bought lunches each day and multiplied it by a full working year, you'd be mortified by how many handbags you'd spent on takeaway food. Get kitchen and wallet savvy and make your own. This £2 lunch is packed full of flavour, is health conscious and is going to get you one step closer to the heels you spotted in that shop window.

SERVES 1

½ tbsp olive oil

2 cloves of garlic, peeled and crushed

a 1cm piece of fresh ginger, peeled and finely chopped

2 spring onions, trimmed and roughly chopped

1 skinless chicken thigh, chopped

2 large, medium-heat fresh red chillies, roughly chopped

1 tbsp curry powder

1 tsp cumin

½ tsp turmeric

200g frozen peas

4 okra, roughly chopped

6 green beans

½ tbsp soy

Heat the oil in a wok or frying pan over a medium heat. Add the garlic, ginger and spring onions and fry for a couple of minutes until soft.

Stir in the chicken and fry for 4–5 minutes, until lightly browned. Stir in the chilli and spices and then add the peas, okra and green beans. Give everything a good stir and pour in the soy and 250ml of water. Leave to simmer for 10 minutes, until nicely thickened. Leave to cool before packing into your lunch box. Keep in the fridge overnight.

Everyone I know dreads mornings, and that's usually because we're all so rushed. People seem to forget about having that much needed 'you time' before work. Preparing a packed lunch is perfect thinking time, whether that's tossing salad or preparing a soup. Use those 15 minutes to really embrace and inspire your day ahead.

CHICKEN AND BACON CHOW MEIN

387
CALORIES
18.4g
FAT
2.7g
SAT FAT
5g
SUGAR
2.3g
SALT

Chicken chow mein is probably one of the most frequently ordered dishes from a UK Chinese takeaway. But, as we all know, the dish can vary in flavour depending on where you buy it. This is down to a few things: how much oil is used, how much seasoning is added, and which type of noodle. Why not guarantee its taste by cooking it yourself at home? My favourite mein to use is a fresh, light egg noodle; it holds its consistency much longer and, because it's not dried, it doesn't soak up the oil, making it a much healthier dish when cooked at home. I've cooked this with both chicken and bacon, as they complement each other well, but as with all the recipes in the book, you can use whatever you have available.

SERVES 2

1 tbsp rice bran oil or vegetable oil

2 rashers of rindless unsmoked back bacon, fat removed, sliced into 1cm strips

150g skinless chicken breast, sliced into 1cm strips

1 leek, trimmed, washed and chopped into 1cm rounds

2 cloves of garlic, peeled and finely chopped

50g frozen peas

250g ready-to-wok egg noodles (or rehydrate the dry variety)

150g bean sprouts

2 tbsp shaosing or dry sherry

1 tbsp light soy sauce

2 tbsp pine nuts

Heat the oil in a wok over a medium to high heat. When hot, add the strips of bacon and stir-fry for 1 minute before increasing the heat as high as it will go and adding the chicken. Stir-fry for 2 minutes, by which time the meat should have started to colour and be almost cooked through.

Reduce the heat a little, add the leek and garlic and stir-fry for 1 minute. Tip in the frozen peas and continue to stir-fry for a further 2 minutes.

Add the noodles and bean sprouts and toss together. Pour in the shaosing and let it bubble up and almost totally evaporate before adding the soy sauce. Mix well, then scatter over the pine nuts. Leave to cool and then pack into a lunch box to eat tomorrow. Keep it in the fridge overnight.

276
CALORIES
9.3g
FAT
2g
SAT FAT
8.1g
SUGAR
3.1g
SALT

FUJIEN-STYLE NOODLES

These noodles come from one of the southernmost areas of China. Often thought to be a Malaysian dish, it was actually taken over to Malaysia by Chinese emigrants. I don't really care who lays claim to it; all I know is that it's delicious and, I warn you now, almost addictive. Serve up these delicious noodles for dinner but keep some back to take for lunch the next day.

SERVES 4

4 tbsp dark soy sauce

1½ tbsp light soy sauce

2 tsp sugar

2 fresh red chillies, deseeded and finely diced

3 tbsp rice bran oil or vegetable oil

400g skinless, boneless chicken thighs, chopped into bite-sized pieces

5 cloves of garlic, peeled and finely chopped

6 spring onions, trimmed, chopped in half and bashed

300g mange tout

400g thick ready-to-wok egg noodles (or rehydrate the dry version)

Mix together the soy sauces, sugar and chopped chilli in a bowl and leave to one side while you cook the rest of the ingredients.

Heat half of the oil in a wok over a very high heat. When hot, add the chicken pieces and stir-fry for 3–4 minutes, until the chicken has browned and is virtually cooked through. Scrape the chicken on to a plate.

Wipe out the wok with some kitchen roll, pour in the remaining oil and place back over the high heat. When the oil is hot, add the garlic, spring onions and mange tout. Stir-fry for 2 minutes and then return the chicken to the wok. Stir-fry for a further minute then toss in the noodles. Pour over the dressing and mix to coat the noodles. The noodles will be a lovely, rich, dark colour – so dark in fact that we often call these chocolate noodles. Either eat immediately or leave to cool and pack into a lunch box. Keep in the fridge overnight.

247
CALORIES
5.1g
FAT
0.8g
SAT FAT
5.6g
SUGAR
3.4g
SALT

KOREAN SEAWEED SALAD

There will come a time when your adventurous side convinces you to look beyond the specialist shelves of your regular grocery shop and into the weird and wondrous world of your local Asian supermarket: a place of hyper-coloured packaging and bizarrely named ingredients. When this time arrives, look no further than my Korean seaweed salad to make the most of your trip to this brave new world. This dish goes particularly well with the tempura vegetables on page 102.

SERVES 2

2 tbsp Korean chilli paste

3 tbsp rice wine vinegar

2 tsp sesame oil

300g cooked and cooled soba noodles

1 tbsp light soy sauce

½ a cucumber, peeled, halved lengthways and deseeded, finely sliced into long lengths

15g dried wakame seaweed, rehydrated in cold water and drained

2 tsp toasted sesame seeds, to serve

Spoon the magical Korean chilli paste into a bowl and pour over the vinegar and sesame oil. Mix well until the ingredients are completely combined.

Place the cooked and cooled noodles in another bowl, pour over the soy sauce and mix together. Add the sliced cucumber and seaweed and pour over the chilli dressing. Mix until everything is well coated (usually I would suggest mixing it with your hands, but this time use spoons so you don't get covered in chilli sauce).

Divide the salad between serving plates and sprinkle with the sesame seeds. Sit back and enjoy your foodie walk on the wild side. If you're making this to eat later, pack into a lunch box and keep in the fridge overnight.

PACKED LUNCH RICE BALLS

392
CALORIES
16.7g
FAT
3.2g
SAT FAT
3.4g
SUGAR
1.9g
SALT

We have a love affair with sandwiches that dates back centuries. The concept of sandwiching a delicious filling between two slabs of bread is endlessly versatile and, as such, is hard to beat. Well, I'm going to have a bloody good go at it! I've made this recipe using creamy mashed avocado, but fillings are only limited by your imagination. Leftovers from almost any of the recipes in this book will make your next lunchtime a treat.

MAKES 4

2 avocados, stone removed, peeled

1 fresh red chilli, deseeded and finely diced

¼ of a red onion, peeled and finely diced

2 tsp fish sauce

2 tsp sesame oil

juice of 1 lime

1 x portion of sushi rice (see page 204)

3 tbsp black sesame seeds

white pepper

Lightly mash the avocado in a bowl with a fork. Mix in the chilli, onion, fish sauce, sesame oil and lime juice and season with a little pepper.

Line the inside of a mug with cling film. (It doesn't have to be perfect, but the cling film should come out over the top of the mug.) Spoon almost a quarter of the rice into the bottom of the lined mug. Using your fingers, push the rice up the sides of the mug until it comes about halfway up, leaving a base of rice at the bottom. Spoon a quarter of the avocado mixture into the mug, then drop another small amount of rice on top to seal.

Gather up the cling film and pull it out of the mug with the rice-covered filling in the bottom. Gently squeeze the cling film around the rice to begin shaping it into a ball. Wet your hands with a little water, carefully remove the rice from the cling film and then press it together with your hands. Roll the ball in the black sesame seeds before repeating the process with the remaining rice and avocado mixture.

Wrap up a ball or two in cling film and pop into your lunch box. Keep refrigerated until ready to eat.

ASIAN-INSPIRED
CURRIES

We've all done it: several sheets to the wind, a zigzag stagger home and before you've had time to unclip your bow tie you're on the blower to the local curry shop. Not-so shiny containers filled with ladles of oil and, at times, unrecognizable ingredients. And there's nothing wrong with that on occasion, but have you ever had the urge to release your inner balti and whip up a vat of your own delicious, heavily spiced curry?

Wherever you land in Asia, there is always a curry waiting for you, with arms outstretched and a smile that could melt the biggest spice cynic's heart – whether it's a laksa in Malaysia, a katsu in Japan or a coconut cream-based beauty in Thailand. And the reason why Asia is so famous for its curries is quite simply because they are so easy to share around the table. More often than not you need no more than fluffy white rice as an accompaniment and it's as satisfying as a Sunday roast.

What I love about curries is that you can adapt them to suit your tastes. The heat volume is controlled by the chilli, the depth managed by the spices, and, whether you want beef, chicken or fish, it's entirely up to you. Once you've mastered the curries in this chapter, I guarantee these will become your go-to dishes when you want to impress, share or love around your dinner table.

658 CALORIES
15.2g FAT
4.4g SAT FAT
7.1g SUGAR
1.8g SALT

BEEF CURRY

Both the Japanese and Koreans favour a curry that more closely resembles chip-shop curry sauce than a curry from an Indian restaurant. It may not sound particularly sophisticated (it's not), but it is unbelievably moreish. I have used short ribs of beef because they become deliciously tender as they slowly cook. However, normal stewing steak works almost as well.

SERVES 6

3 tbsp rice bran oil or vegetable oil

10 x short beef ribs (about 1.8kg in total, including bone weight), trimmed of fat

2 red onions, peeled and roughly chopped

2 carrots, peeled and chopped into 1cm dice

a 5cm piece of fresh ginger, peeled and minced or grated

5 cloves of garlic, peeled and minced or grated

2 tbsp curry powder

2 star anise

2 tbsp dark soy sauce

700ml hot, light beef or chicken stock

3 potatoes, peeled and chopped into rough 5cm pieces

300g frozen peas

600g steamed white rice

3 large flatbreads (see page 198), to serve

Heat 1 tablespoon of the oil in a large saucepan over a high heat. When hot, add the ribs and fry for about 4 minutes, turning, until golden all over. You may need to do this in batches depending on the size of your pan. Once browned, transfer the ribs to a plate. Wipe out the pan with some kitchen roll.

Blitz the onions to a purée in a food processor. Heat the remaining oil in the pan over a medium to high heat and fry the onion paste for about 8 minutes, stirring regularly, until it has softened a little and taken on some colour.

Add the carrots, ginger and garlic, and continue to stir-fry for a further 2–3 minutes before adding the curry powder and star anise. Fry for another minute.

Tip the browned ribs back into the pan and stir to coat in the spicy mixture before pouring in the soy sauce and hot stock. Bring to the boil and then reduce the heat and simmer for about 1½ hours, until the meat is incredibly tender.

Add the potato pieces and simmer for a further 10 minutes or so, until cooked. Stir in the peas, and let them heat through for 2 minutes. Serve with the rice and half a flatbread each.

760 CALORIES
41.9g FAT
21.7g SAT FAT
4.1g SUGAR
1.6g SALT

LAMB RENDANG

This is a traditional Malaysian curry that pulls no punches in terms of flavour. The classic version is made with beef, but this is my take on it using lamb. The addition of just a small amount of desiccated coconut at the end adds depth to the dish and a lovely subtle texture.

SERVES 4

4cm fresh galangal, peeled and roughly chopped, or 2 heaped tsp from a jar

2 tsp crushed dried chillies

3 dry Kaffir lime leaves

a 3cm piece of fresh ginger, peeled and roughly chopped

4 cloves of garlic, peeled and roughly chopped

2 cardamom pods

2 tbsp rice bran oil or vegetable oil

800g extra-lean diced lamb leg

1 large red onion, peeled and roughly sliced

1 stick of cinnamon, broken in half

1 x 400ml tin of light coconut milk

1 tbsp dark soy sauce

1 tbsp light soy sauce

2 tbsp desiccated coconut

4 tbsp chopped fresh coriander

salt and white pepper

400g steamed jasmine rice, to serve

Place the galangal, crushed chillies, lime leaves, ginger, garlic and cardamom in a pestle and mortar. Add a splash of warm water and season with a little salt and pepper. Pound the ingredients to a smooth paste, then leave to one side.

Heat half the oil in a wok over a high heat. Season the lamb with salt and pepper and then carefully drop it into the hot oil. Fry for 2–3 minutes, until golden all over. Tip the meat into a sieve standing over a bowl to drain away any excess fat.

Wipe the wok with some kitchen roll. Place it back over a medium to high heat and pour in the remaining tablespoon of oil. Add the onion and the cinnamon and fry for 3 minutes, just until the onion begins to lose its shape. Stir in the curry paste from the pestle and mortar and continue to fry, stirring regularly, for 2 minutes.

Tip the drained meat back into the pan and stir to coat. Pour in the coconut milk and the soy sauces and mix gently.

Cook the rendang, uncovered, for about 40 minutes, until the liquid has reduced by half and the meat is meltingly tender. Stir through the desiccated coconut and the coriander just before serving with steamed jasmine rice.

FILIPINO PORK AND MANGO CURRY

446
CALORIES
11.8g
FAT
3.7g
SAT FAT
14g
SUGAR
1.2g
SALT

Like wearing six-inch heels, this dish is all about perfect balance. The combination of sweet mangoes and sour vinegar gives the curry an unusual and surprising taste experience that you'll definitely want to revisit.

SERVES 4

1½ tbsp rice bran oil or vegetable oil

800g trimmed pork loin, chopped into 3cm chunks

2 small red onions, peeled and finely sliced

3 cloves of garlic, peeled and finely chopped

a 3cm piece of fresh ginger, peeled and finely chopped

2 fresh red chillies, finely chopped

1 tbsp curry powder

2 tsp ground cinnamon

2 tsp ground nutmeg

2 mangoes, peeled and chopped into 2cm chunks

50ml red wine vinegar

1 tbsp soy sauce

2 tbsp agave nectar, palm sugar or dark brown sugar

salt and white pepper

300g boiled rice, to serve

coriander, to serve

Heat half the oil in a wok over a high heat. Season the pork with a little salt and pepper. When the oil is hot, add the pork and stir-fry for 2 minutes until browned all over. Transfer the pork to a plate.

Wipe the wok with some kitchen roll. Place it back over a medium to high heat and pour in the remaining tablespoon of oil. Add the onions, garlic, ginger and chillies and stir-fry for 3 minutes.

Sprinkle in the curry powder, cinnamon and nutmeg and stir-fry for 1 minute. Add the mango chunks, vinegar, soy sauce and the agave nectar along with half a glass of water (about 125ml). Bring the mixture to the boil and then reduce the heat and simmer for 5 minutes.

Return the seared pork to the wok and mix well to coat in the sauce. Continue to simmer the curry for a further 5 minutes. Serve the curry garnished with coriander, alongside a mountain of fluffy rice.

393
CALORIES
7.9g
FAT
1.6g
SAT FAT
6.6g
SUGAR
1.4g
SALT

CHICKEN KATSU CURRY

This dish is perfect to serve up to any of your friends who say they don't like Asian food. It's probably one of the most mainstream dishes available in the UK. A light, fruity sauce with strips of chicken coated in breadcrumbs and baked in the oven.

SERVES 4

2 x 175g chicken breasts, sliced in half horizontally
2 egg whites
120g dry breadcrumbs
1 tbsp rice bran oil or olive oil
white pepper
400g steamed brown rice, to serve

FOR THE SAUCE

1 tbsp rice bran oil or vegetable oil
1 small onion, peeled and very finely chopped
3 cloves of garlic, peeled and very finely chopped
a 1cm piece of fresh ginger, peeled and finely chopped
1 tbsp mild curry powder
200ml hot, light vegetable stock
75ml apple juice
½ tbsp fish sauce
2 tsp cornflour mixed with a little water to form a paste
a pinch of sugar
white pepper

Preheat the grill to its highest setting. Line a baking tray with greaseproof paper.

Season the chicken breast pieces on both sides with a little white pepper. Lightly whisk the egg whites in a shallow bowl until frothy. Spread out the breadcrumbs on a plate.

Dip each piece of chicken breast first in the egg whites and then in the breadcrumbs. Press the breadcrumbs into the meat to coat evenly and thoroughly. Place the crumbed chicken on the lined baking tray.

Drizzle the chicken with a little oil and grill for about 4 minutes on each side, until golden and cooked through.

Meanwhile, make the sauce. Heat the oil in a small saucepan over a medium heat. Once hot, add the onion, garlic and ginger. Fry for 3–4 minutes, stirring frequently, until the onions are soft. Sprinkle over the curry powder and fry for 1 minute before pouring in the hot stock and the apple juice. Bring the mixture up to the boil and simmer until it has reduced by a quarter.

Mix in the fish sauce and cornflour paste, and stir until the sauce thickens. Season with white pepper and a pinch of sugar, then serve the crispy chicken breasts with the sauce spooned over the top and the rice alongside.

735
CALORIES
27.7g
FAT
16.9g
SAT·FAT
5.3g
SUGAR
2g
SALT

EASY LAKSA

My best friend E'lain was born and raised in Singapore . . . thank goodness! Over the last ten years, I've been lucky enough to visit Singapore with her and eat like a true Singaporean. I love the upscale hawker markets with their lane upon lane and stall upon stall of the best food Asia has to offer. One dish I'll always hunt out like a bloodhound is a Malaysian laksa. As far as I'm concerned, this dish is the princess of the curry world: polite, fragrant, simple and modest. The flavours are a perfect blend of coconut and light spice, and even the chilli is a mere hint. Nothing like you'd find in a king balti. For any curry virgins out there, I urge you to add this dish to your repertoire.

SERVES 2

1 tsp rice bran oil or vegetable oil

3cm fresh galangal, peeled and finely chopped, or 2 tsp from a jar

a 2cm piece of fresh ginger, peeled and finely chopped

2 cloves of garlic, peeled and finely chopped

1 stalk of lemon grass, trimmed and finely chopped

2 fresh red chillies, split lengthways

1 tsp curry powder

1 tsp turmeric

2 Kaffir lime leaves

2 small tomatoes roughly chopped into 2cm chunks

200ml hot vegetable stock

1 x 400ml tin of light coconut milk

150g skinless salmon fillet, chopped into rough 2cm chunks

8 raw king prawns, shelled

2 tsp fish sauce

200g vermicelli noodles, soaked according to the packet instructions

optional: fresh coriander leaves, to serve

Heat the oil in a wok over a medium to high heat. When hot, add the galangal, ginger, garlic, lemon grass and chillies and stir-fry for 2 minutes. Sprinkle over the curry powder and turmeric, and continue to fry for 30 seconds before adding the lime leaves and tomatoes. Fry the mixture for 2–3 minutes, until the tomatoes begin to break down. Pour in the hot stock and the coconut milk. Give everything a stir, then bring the mixture to the boil. Reduce the heat and let the soup simmer for 10 minutes to allow the flavours to infuse.

Add the salmon chunks and the prawns to the soup with the fish sauce. Simmer gently for about 2 minutes, until cooked through.

Divide the noodles between serving bowls, pour over the hot laksa and scatter with coriander leaves, if using.

462
CALORIES

17.1g
FAT

12.1g
SAT FAT

5.8g
SUGAR

4.1g
SALT

THAI GREEN CURRY

I am always disappointed when I flick through recipe books to see Thai curries that lazily list shop-bought pastes. Sure, there are some brilliant pastes available that are a shortcut to a quick meal, but they already have a recipe on the side of the pot! So, here's my recipe. I've conjured up the flavour with readily available ingredients, so it may not be 100 per cent authentic, but it is absolutely 100 per cent delicious.

SERVES 4

6 shallots, peeled and roughly chopped

10 green bird's eye chillies (reduce the number of chillies if you don't like it too hot)

50g fresh coriander, stems and all, roughly chopped

20g fresh basil, stems and all, roughly chopped

2 stalks of lemon grass, trimmed and roughly chopped

4cm fresh galangal, peeled and roughly chopped, or 2 heaped tsp from a jar

2 tinned anchovy fillets, drained and roughly chopped

5 cloves of garlic, peeled and roughly chopped

juice and zest of 1 lime

3 tbsp fish sauce

150g coconut cream

400g skinless chicken breast, chopped into bite-sized chunks

300g aubergine, trimmed and chopped into bite-sized chunks

250ml hot chicken or vegetable stock

500g steamed jasmine rice, to serve

¼ fresh red chilli, to serve

Blitz the shallots, chillies, coriander, basil, lemon grass, galangal, anchovies, garlic, lime zest and 2 tablespoons of the fish sauce in a small food processor until you achieve a fairly smooth paste. (You can also do this with a pestle and mortar.)

Spoon the coconut cream into a wok and heat over a medium to high heat for a couple of minutes; it will melt, boil and then begin to split. When it has split, stir in the curry paste. Cook for 2 minutes, stirring frequently.

Add the chicken and aubergine and stir gently for 2 minutes, by which time they should be well coated in the sauce.

Pour in the hot stock and simmer for about 10 minutes, or until the chicken is cooked through and the aubergine is soft, while still holding its shape. Serve the curry with freshly steamed jasmine rice sprinkled with chopped red chilli.

SWEET POTATO AND BRAZIL NUT CURRY

456
CALORIES
19.1g
FAT
8g
SAT FAT
14.1g
SUGAR
1.4g
SALT

There are very few countries in the world where vegetarian food is as important as it is in Asia. The Buddhist culture of many Asian regions means that lots of people often choose vegetarian food over meat-based meals and this curry makes a great veggie alternative to the lamb rendang on page 74. If you have any leftovers, take them to work to eat with pitta bread for lunch, or blitz them with a drained can of chickpeas and stir in a little sour cream or crème fraîche. This is a great curry to serve on a flatbread (see page 198), which will mop up all the juices, but you can easily serve it with a bowl of steaming rice.

SERVES 4

500g sweet potatoes, peeled and chopped into chunks

1 tbsp rice bran oil or vegetable oil

2 small red onions, peeled and chopped into large dice

a 3cm piece of fresh ginger, peeled and finely chopped

5 cloves of garlic, peeled and finely chopped

1 red pepper, deseeded and chopped into 2cm pieces

½ tbsp ground cinnamon

½ tbsp Chinese five spice

½ tbsp ground turmeric

1 tsp chilli powder

200ml light coconut milk

1 tbsp dark soy sauce

1 tbsp light soy sauce

3 tbsp desiccated coconut

50g Brazil nuts, roughly chopped

400g cooked white rice, to serve

4 tbsp fat-free Greek yoghurt, to serve

1 tbsp fresh coriander leaves, to serve

Place the sweet potato in a large pan of water, bring to the boil and cook for about 10–15 minutes until tender. Drain well.

Heat the oil in a wok over a medium to high heat. When hot, tumble in the onions, ginger, garlic and red pepper. Fry for 2 minutes, stirring often, before sprinkling in all the spices. Continue to fry for a further 30 seconds to lightly cook the spices. Add the coconut milk and give the mixture a stir.

Add a splash of water to loosen the ingredients, then tip in the cooked sweet potato and stir to combine and warm through.

Gently stir in both of the soy sauces, the desiccated coconut and the chopped Brazil nuts. Serve the curry topped with Greek yoghurt and chopped coriander.

172
CALORIES
9.1g
FAT
3g
SAT FAT
7.4g
SUGAR
0.7g
SALT

OKRA AND BUTTERBEAN CURRY

You *can* buy pre-mixed spice blends, but why not make your own? It's really not difficult and you can experiment with the flavours you love to make it personal to you. To make this a meaty dish, add some cooked roast chicken at the beginning when you stir-fry the spices.

SERVES 4

2 tbsp rice bran oil or vegetable oil

1 red onion, peeled and finely diced

4 cloves of garlic, peeled and finely chopped

a 3cm piece of fresh ginger, peeled and finely chopped

2 fresh red chillies, finely chopped (deseeded if you don't like it too hot)

1 tsp ground cinnamon

½ tsp ground cloves

2 tsp Chinese five spice

2 star anise, lightly crushed

300g okra, rinsed and trimmed

3 tomatoes, roughly chopped

1 x 420g tin of butterbeans, rinsed and drained

4 heaped tbsp fat-free Greek yoghurt, to serve

fresh coriander, to garnish

Heat the oil in a wok over a medium heat. When hot, add the onion and cook for 5 minutes, stirring frequently. Increase the heat, add the garlic, ginger and chillies and stir-fry for 2 minutes.

Add the ground spices and star anise, and continue to fry for a further 30 seconds, stirring almost constantly. Add the okra, tomatoes and a splash of water. Bring the mixture to the boil and then reduce the heat. Place a lid on top and cook for about 15 minutes, until the tomatoes have broken down and the okra is tender. Keep an eye on it and add a little extra water if it looks like it might be drying out.

Stir in the butterbeans and cook for 5 minutes. Serve with a dollop of Greek yoghurt and garnished with coriander.

 TIP: If you have any leftovers, they can be processed with a little extra warm water to make a delicious soup. Reheat until piping hot.

DINNER PARTIES

Show me someone who doesn't love a dinner party and I'll show you a liar. I love hosting a dinner party nearly as much as I love going to one. Dressing the table, cooking the food and serving drinks is almost as enjoyable as the eating – I DID SAY ALMOST! I've been known to spend days pondering over a menu, creating the perfect culinary performance for my guests, and I love showing off about what I've done.

For me, hosting a dinner party is not dissimilar to staging a West End play. The table becomes your set, the menu your script and the dishes your actors; it is a spellbinding narration of food. Depending on who's coming round, I may put on a Dickensian classic of 12 well-written dishes, or a fun two-course farce ... whichever it is, this chapter will undoubtedly get you a standing ovation.

Preparation is key. Never rush yourself. If you're short on time, don't try to stretch yourself too thin – keep it simple. Your guests will love whatever you serve and they will love it even more if you're relaxed ... after all, they are here to see you!

616
CALORIES
17.2g
FAT
4.2g
SAT FAT
13.1g
SUGAR
3.8g
SALT

PORK BAHN MI

It has been known for Asian families to dine for over four hours at one sitting. It really is the best way to eat. In the Asian community this tends to happen on Sundays because many Asian families work in catering and Sunday lunch is one of the only times during the week that the takeaways and restaurants are closed. Sunday lunches for Family Wan were sacred. We would all sit around a large round table, either at home or in my Auntie Maureen's restaurant, and eat our way through the day. Chinese tea would be served in little teacups and Dad would tell us stories from his village in Hong Kong (most of them we had heard before but we never told Dad!). Food really did bring our family together and I hope it always will.

MAKES ENOUGH FOR 4 LARGE FLATBREADS

800g trimmed pork loin, sliced into 1cm slices

2 tbsp agave nectar or honey

3 tbsp fish sauce

1 tbsp soy sauce

a 3cm piece of fresh ginger, peeled and finely chopped

2 carrots, peeled and finely chopped into matchsticks

1 cucumber, peeled, halved lengthways and deseeded, chopped into 0.5cm pieces

3 tbsp rice wine vinegar

4 tbsp light mayonnaise

1 tbsp sweet chilli sauce

2 tbsp rice bran oil or vegetable oil

4 large flatbreads, to serve (see page 198)

¼ of a white cabbage, shredded, to serve

lime wedges, to serve

fresh mint and coriander leaves, to serve

Place the pork slices in a large bowl. Pour over half of the agave nectar, 2 tablespoons of the fish sauce, all of the soy sauce and the chopped ginger. Mix well, making sure all the meat is thoroughly coated. Leave to marinate in the fridge for at least 30 minutes, or overnight.

Place the carrots and cucumber in a bowl and pour over the vinegar and the remaining agave nectar and fish sauce.

Mix together the mayonnaise and the chilli sauce.

Heat the oil in a wok over a medium to high heat. When hot, add the pork and stir-fry for 3–4 minutes, until nicely browned all over and cooked through.

Spread a little chilli mayonnaise over each flatbread and top with some pork and pickled cucumber and carrot. Finish with some of the shredded white cabbage and drizzle with the remaining chilli mayonnaise. Serve with a wedge of lime to squeeze over the top.

BULGOGI BEEF WRAP

Sitting around a table and sharing a meal with the people you love is one of life's great joys. I like to serve these beef wraps alongside the pork bahn mi and the prawn and tomatoes (see pages 92 and 94). Tear off pieces of flatbread and use them to dip into the different bowls of food. It's like Asian tapas!

MAKES ENOUGH FOR 4 LARGE FLATBREADS

800g trimmed sirloin beef steak, sliced into 1cm slices

4 spring onions, trimmed and finely sliced

a 3cm piece of fresh ginger, peeled and very finely chopped

3 cloves of garlic, peeled and very finely chopped

5 tbsp soy sauce

2 tbsp rice wine vinegar

2 tsp agave nectar or honey

2 tsp sesame oil

¼ of a white cabbage, shredded

1 small carrot, peeled and finely chopped into matchsticks

2 tbsp rice bran oil or vegetable oil

white pepper

4 large flatbreads, to serve (see page 198)

Place the beef, spring onions, ginger, garlic, a good pinch of white pepper and 4 tablespoons of soy sauce in a bowl. Mix thoroughly and leave in the fridge to marinate for at least 30 minutes, or overnight.

Mix together the remaining tablespoon of soy sauce, the vinegar, agave nectar and sesame oil. Place the shredded cabbage and carrot in a large bowl and pour over the dressing. Mix to coat and then keep to one side.

Heat the oil in a wok over a high heat. When hot, add the marinated beef. Stir-fry for 2–3 minutes, until the meat is nicely coloured and just cooked through.

Place the meat along the middle of each flatbread, top with some of the Asian coleslaw and wrap up and eat with your hands.

406
CALORIES
9.4g
FAT
1.5g
SAT FAT
7.7g
SUGAR
3.7g
SALT

PRAWN AND TOMATOES

When it comes to planning a menu, it's all about balance. Rather than serving one main dish, have a few on the table so your guests can try a bit of everything. These sweet, juicy prawns are perfect eaten alongside a meatier dish or even a crunchy salad. You can leave in the chilli seeds if you fancy something a little more fiery.

MAKES ENOUGH FOR 4 LARGE
FLATBREADS

1 tbsp rice bran oil or vegetable oil

4 spring onions, trimmed and chopped
into 1cm pieces

2 cloves of garlic, peeled and finely
chopped

2 fresh red chillies, deseeded and
finely chopped

450g raw king prawns

a splash of shaosing or dry sherry

3 tomatoes, deseeded and roughly
chopped into 2cm pieces

2 tbsp soy sauce

2 tsp fish sauce

2 tbsp tomato ketchup

2 tsp sesame oil

4 large flatbreads, to serve (see page
198)

½ an iceberg lettuce, shredded, to
serve

Heat the oil in a wok over a medium to high heat. When hot, add the spring onions, garlic and chillies. Stir-fry for 1 minute before turning up the heat as high as it will go and adding the prawns. Stir-fry for a further minute.

Pour in the shaosing and let it bubble off and almost completely evaporate before adding the tomato pieces. Stir-fry for 2 minutes, until the tomatoes are just beginning to soften. Remove the wok from the heat and stir in the soy sauce, fish sauce, tomato ketchup and sesame oil.

Pile the prawns and tomatoes on to your flatbreads, top with shredded lettuce and get stuck in.

NOTE: This is a recipe from my childhood that my Dad used to cook for us all the time. Everyone always asks how to make it, and the secret is tomato ketchup. It's the perfect combination of East meets West.

149
CALORIES
2.2g
FAT
0.5g
SAT FAT
0.9g
SUGAR
1.3g
SALT

PRAWN AND DILL FLAT PANCAKES

I've never been shy of rolling up my sleeves and getting involved. Dad taught me that as a child. 'You can do,' Dad would say in his comedy accent! And 'DO' I did . . . These pancakes are what I call a 'Do' dish; there are no two ways about it, you have to get stuck in! Roll up those perfectly tailored sleeves, throw flour everywhere and release that inner child! Once you've made your dumpling, you squash it into a pancake. You can think about whatever or whomever you like when squashing . . . ENJOY!

MAKES 8

1 x quantity of flatbread dough
(see page 198)
flour, to dust
300g raw, peeled king prawns, very
finely chopped (almost minced)
3 tbsp finely chopped fresh dill
1 tbsp shaosing or dry sherry
2 tsp fish sauce
6 bamboo shoots, finely chopped
6 water chestnuts, finely chopped
4 tsp rice bran oil or vegetable oil
salt and white pepper
lemon wedges, to serve

Divide the flatbread dough into
8 evenly sized pieces and, on a
clean surface dusted with a little
flour, roll out one piece of dough to
a circle about 15cm in diameter.

SMASH!!!

ROLL!!!

CHOP!!!

Place all the remaining ingredients apart from the oil and lemon wedges in a bowl. Add a generous amount of white pepper and a little salt. Mix well to combine.

Place 1 heaped tablespoon (one-eighth) of the prawn mixture in a small mound in the centre of the rolled-out dough. Draw the edges of the dough into the middle so that they are overlapping and pinch and twist the top of the dough to seal. Flip the parcel over so that the join is underneath.

Using your hands, gently but firmly pat the pancake around the sides to form a scone shape, then flatten down with the palm of your hand. Repeat the process of turning and patting until your pancake is about 10–12cm in diameter. Don't worry if little bits of the filling escape through the dough; these will go lovely and crispy when you cook them. Place your finished pancake to one side while you repeat the process with the remaining dough and filling.

 TIP: Serve the warm pancakes on their own for a delicious snack, or with a salad for a more complete meal.

When your pancakes are ready to cook, heat a large non-stick frying pan over a medium to high heat. When hot, drizzle in a little oil (you will need to cook the pancakes in a single layer, so allow half a teaspoon of oil per pancake and cook them in batches). When the oil is hot, fry the pancakes for 3 minutes on each side, until the dough is browned and blistered in some areas, and the prawns are fully cooked. (The only way to make sure they are cooked is by breaking one open and having a look. The prawns should be a lovely pink colour and the pancake should release a little steam.) Repeat with the rest of the pancakes and serve hot or cold with a wedge of lemon.

PORK AND CHIVE FLAT PANCAKES

This recipe is a meatier variation of the prawn and dill recipe on page 96. Once you've mastered the technique, have a go at experimenting with your own flavour combinations.

MAKES 8

400g lean pork mince

4 tbsp chopped fresh chives

a 3cm piece of fresh ginger, peeled and grated

3 cloves of garlic, peeled and finely chopped

1 x quantity of flatbread dough (see page 198)

flour, to dust

1 tbsp light soy sauce

4 tsp of rice bran oil or vegetable oil

salt and white pepper

Place the pork, chives, ginger and garlic in a bowl and season with salt and pepper. Mix well with your hands.

Divide the flatbread dough into 8 even pieces. Dust your work surface with a little flour and roll out one piece of dough to a circle about 15cm in diameter.

Place 1 heaped tablespoon of the pork mixture in a small mound in the centre of the rolled-out dough. Draw the edges of the dough into the middle so that they are overlapping and pinch together to seal. Flip the parcel over so that the join is underneath.

Using your hands, gently but firmly pat the pancake around the sides to form a scone shape, then flatten down with the palm of your hand. Repeat the process of turning and patting until your pancake is about 10–12cm in diameter. Don't worry if little bits of the filling escape through the dough; these will go lovely and crispy when you cook them. Place your finished pancake to one side while you repeat the process with the remaining dough and filling.

Heat a large non-stick frying pan over a medium to high heat. When hot, drizzle in a little oil (you will need to cook the pancakes in a single layer, so allow half a teaspoon of oil per pancake and cook them in batches). When the oil is hot, fry the pancakes for 4–5 minutes on each side, until the dough is browned and blistered in some areas, and the pork is fully cooked through. (The only sure way to make sure the pork is cooked is by breaking open one of your pancakes and having a look.) Serve while still warm.

322
CALORIES
12.2g
FAT
1.5g
SAT FAT
8.6g
SUGAR
1.1g
SALT

TEMPURA VEGETABLES WITH PANCAKES

This dish is made with the type of pancakes that you would usually use to roll up shredded crispy duck, so it is my crunchy vegetarian alternative to everyone's favourite Chinese finger food. The pancakes are so filling, though, that you'll never miss the meat.

SERVES 6

100g plain white flour

100g cornflour

300ml sparkling water

1 small potato, peeled and finely sliced into matchsticks

2 carrots, peeled and finely sliced into matchsticks

1 courgette, trimmed and finely sliced into matchsticks

1 red onion, peeled and finely diced

vegetable oil, to deep-fry

18 Peking-style pancakes

6 tbsp hoisin sauce

6 spring onions, trimmed and finely sliced

1 cucumber, peeled, halved lengthways and deseeded, finely sliced into matchsticks

salt

Tip both the flours into a bowl and whisk in enough of the sparkling water to make a batter with the consistency of single cream (you may not need all the water). Season with a little salt.

Place the prepared potato, carrots, courgette and onion in a bowl and mix together.

Pour the vegetable oil into a large heavy-based saucepan to a depth of about 10cm. Heat over a medium heat to 180°C (if you don't have a kitchen thermometer, test the temperature of the oil by dropping in a small cube of white bread; it should turn golden brown in about 10 seconds). Preheat the oven to 20°C/50°F/Gas mark ⅛.

Drop the vegetables into the batter and mix together so that they are roughly coated.

The next bit takes a little practice, but I promise you will get the hang of it. Use your fingers to pick up a small amount of the batter-coated vegetables; they should be dripping with the batter. Carefully drop the vegetables into the hot oil. The batter should begin cooking, immediately welding the vegetables together; don't worry too much if some float astray. Repeat until you have a few tempura vegetable parcels floating on the surface of the oil. Do not overload the oil, as it will reduce the temperature and result in soggy, oily tempura.

Fry the vegetables for about 3 minutes, until they are firm when tapped with a metal spoon and are a light golden colour. Transfer the tempura to kitchen roll to drain off any excess oil, then keep them warm on a baking tray in the oven while you repeat the process with the remaining vegetables.

When ready to serve, steam the pancakes for a couple of minutes in a steamer basket set over a pan of boiling water. Spread a little hoisin over each pancake and top with the tempura, spring onions and cucumber. Roll them up like you would a duck pancake and you will soon be muttering the words, 'Crispy duck who?!'.

MINI SCALLOP AND ANCHOVY SOUFFLÉS

145
CALORIES
9.9g
FAT
2.4g
SAT FAT
0.2g
SUGAR
0.8g
SALT

Everyone needs a dish in the locker that looks far more complicated than it is to cook. Cooking time is minimal here, and everything can be prepped in advance. Throw all the ingredients into your ramekins and leave in the fridge until you're ready to cook. Eaten with tiny teaspoons, your guests will enjoy a five-star dining experience involving only one-star effort.

SERVES 4

- 4 whole eggs, plus 2 whites
- 1 tbsp sesame oil
- 4 spring onions, trimmed and finely sliced
- 4 tinned anchovy fillets, drained and chopped into small pieces
- 4 scallops, roe removed, and quartered
- 4 large raw prawns, peeled and quartered
- 4 small sprigs of fresh coriander, to serve

Beat the eggs and extra whites with the sesame oil, spring onions and chopped anchovies.

Arrange the scallops and prawns evenly in the bottom of four ramekins and pour over the egg mixture.

Place the filled ramekins in a large steamer basket set over a wok of simmering water (make sure the bottom of the steamer doesn't touch the water). Steam for 12–15 minutes, until the egg is firm to the touch. Keep an eye on the water level and top up if needed. Serve each soufflé with a sprig of coriander.

60	CALORIES
3.1g	FAT
0.6g	SAT FAT
1.1g	SUGAR
1g	SALT

VEGGIE GYOZA

You say dumpling; I say gyoza! The main difference between the two is the way they are cooked. Gyozas start off in a frying pan, which gives them a crispy appearance and a distinctive flavour. They may be a little less healthy than boiled or steamed dumplings, but I'm never one to shy away from a little of what you fancy. For these moreish morsels, you can use anything that you have leftover in the fridge, but make sure the ingredients are quite firm and crunchy. Traditionally, the Chinese fry the gyoza again, once they have poached them, but the Japanese don't, which is obviously much healthier.

MAKES 12

12 thick flour wonton wrappers

1 egg, beaten

2 tsp rice bran oil or vegetable oil

2 tbsp soy sauce, to serve

1 tbsp chilli oil, to serve

FOR THE FILLING

100g tinned bamboo shoots, finely chopped

1 spring onion, trimmed and finely sliced

1 tbsp chopped fresh chives

2 tbsp chopped fresh dill

30g unsalted peanuts, roughly chopped

4 water chestnuts, finely chopped

1 small carrot, peeled and finely chopped

½ a courgette, grated

a 1cm piece of fresh ginger, peeled and finely chopped

1 tsp fish sauce

1 tbsp light soy sauce

1 tbsp oyster sauce

½ tsp sesame oil

white pepper

Place all the ingredients for the filling in a bowl and mix well with your hands. Season with a generous amount of white pepper.

Take a wonton wrapper and place a tablespoon of the vegetable mixture in the centre. Using your finger, brush a little egg around the edge of the wrapper. Now you need to seal your dumpling. Hold the wonton flat in the palm of your hand and, using your other hand, draw the closest and furthest edges together and pinch them so that they stick. Carefully seal the remaining edges together, trying to avoid trapping any air in the wonton. Place to one side, and repeat with the rest of the wrappers and the filling.

Heat half of the oil in a wok over a medium to high heat. When hot, place 6 gyoza in the wok and fry for about a minute, until the wrapper has browned and crisped up.

Pour in about 5 tablespoons of water and immediately cover the wok with a lid or large plate. Leave the gyoza to steam cook for 2 minutes before lifting the lid and having a look at how much water there is left. You will need to cook the dumplings for another 2 minutes, so it is likely you will have to add a splash more water before clamping on the lid again. This cooking process takes a little practice, as you don't want to waterlog your dumplings, but you also don't want them to burn dry.

Transfer the cooked gyoza to a plate while you cook the rest. Serve dipped in soy sauce and chilli oil.

Tip: When you're using tins of Asian ingredients, drain and keep the ingredients in a plastic tub filled with fresh water. They will keep for several days in the fridge.

429
CALORIES

16g
FAT

2.8g
SAT FAT

3.3g
SUGAR

1g
SALT

MINT AND PISTACHIO SEA BASS

Mint and pistachios work together like shoes and handbags. They perfectly complement each other without working too hard. Sea bass has a very subtle flavour, leaving enough room for the other flavours to do their job.

SERVES 4

100g shelled unsalted pistachio nuts

6 tbsp fresh mint leaves, roughly chopped

6 tbsp fresh coriander leaves, roughly chopped

a 2cm piece of fresh ginger, peeled and roughly chopped

2 cloves of garlic, peeled and chopped

½ tsp ground coriander

½ tsp ground cinnamon

½ tsp ground cardamom

1 heaped tablespoon fat-free Greek yoghurt

2 fresh red chillies, deseeded and roughly chopped

juice of 1 lime

1 tbsp fish sauce

4 x 110g sea bass fillets, scaled and pin-boned

1 tbsp rice bran oil or vegetable oil

white pepper

450g cooked brown rice, to serve

75g watercress, to serve

Place all of the ingredients, apart from the fish, oil, rice and watercress in a small food processor. Season with a little pepper and blitz until you achieve a thick, smooth mixture. If necessary, add a little warm water to help with the processing.

Season your fish fillets with salt and pepper and smother them on both sides with the marinade. Leave the fish to marinate for at least 5 minutes but no more than 30 minutes.

Preheat the grill as high as it will go. Line a baking tray with foil and drizzle with the oil. Lay the fish, skin-side up, on the tray and top with the marinade. Grill for 4 minutes, then turn over carefully and cook for 2–3 minutes on the other side.

Serve your deliciously aromatic fish with virtuous brown rice and watercress.

STEAMED CHICKEN WITH RED DATES AND GOJI BERRIES

Stop the ageing process and protect against cancer – these are just two of the claims the health world makes about goji berries. I can't tell you whether those claims are true, but I can say that most of Asia has been using them as a medicine for centuries. Have a go at this recipe, and, at the very least, you'll have a delicious dinner to eat.

SERVES 4

100ml light soy sauce

480g skinless chicken breast, chopped into large chunks

100g fresh shiitake mushrooms, halved

2 cloves of garlic, peeled and minced or grated

8 dried red dates

50g goji berries

4 spring onions, trimmed, halved and bashed

a 3cm piece of fresh ginger, peeled and finely sliced into matchsticks

2 tbsp shaosing or dry sherry

400g steamed white rice, to serve

2 fresh red chillies, deseeded and finely sliced, to serve

Pour the soy sauce into a bowl along with 100ml of water. Add the chicken, mushrooms and garlic. Give the mixture a good stir and then leave to marinade in the fridge for 45 minutes, or ideally overnight.

Place the dates and goji berries in separate bowls and pour over enough warm water to just cover them. Soak the goji berries for about 15 minutes before draining, and the dates for about 45 minutes. Set aside.

Line the base of a large steamer basket with foil. Drain the chicken and mushrooms (discarding the marinade) and arrange on the foil. Scatter over the rehydrated goji berries, dates, the spring onions and the ginger. Drizzle the shaosing over the meat, then put the lid on the basket and rest over a wok of simmering water. Ensure that the base of the basket is not touching the water. Steam the chicken for about 35 minutes, until it is fully cooked through. Keep an eye on the level of water in the wok, topping up as needed. Spoon the steamed chicken into a bowl with the rest of the contents of the steamer basket. Pour over any juices. Serve with the steamed rice and garnish with the sliced chillies.

324
CALORIES
20.5g
FAT
3.5g
SAT FAT
2.4g
SUGAR
1.5g
SALT

SALMON WITH PEA SHOOTS AND OYSTER SAUCE

Gathering the people you love around you to eat a meal together is something we should all do more often. But throwing a dinner party needn't mean endless lists of ingredients and complicated cooking instructions. Simply cooked salmon with a fresh pea shoot salad is almost effortlessly easy to prepare. Fried shallots, although maybe not all that healthy, deliver wokfuls of flavour – but you can always leave them out if you are feeling especially virtuous.

SERVES 6

1 x 800g skinless salmon fillet

2 tbsp rice bran oil or vegetable oil

a 4cm piece of fresh ginger, peeled and thinly sliced into matchsticks

100ml shaosing or dry sherry

vegetable oil, for deep-frying

6 shallots, peeled and finely sliced

2 tbsp oyster sauce

2 tbsp light soy sauce

8 shiitake mushrooms, trimmed and finely sliced

4 cloves of garlic, peeled and finely sliced

5 spring onions, trimmed and sliced into 1cm pieces

250g pea shoots

salt and white pepper

Preheat the oven to 180°C/350°F/Gas mark 3. Tear off two sheets of foil a little longer than your fish fillet. Lay one sheet on a baking tray and drizzle with some of the rice bran oil. Place the salmon on top. Season with pepper and scatter over the ginger. Place the second piece of foil on top of the salmon and seal the foil on three of the sides; the parcel should be loose with plenty of room around the fish. Pour half of the shaosing into the open end, before sealing that side too. Cook in the oven for 25 minutes. Remove from the oven and leave to rest for 5 minutes.

Pour the vegetable oil into a large heavy-based saucepan to a depth of about 2.5cm. Heat over a medium heat to 170°C (if you don't have a kitchen thermometer, test the temperature of the oil by dropping in a small cube of white bread; it should turn golden brown in about 12 seconds).

Carefully drop the sliced shallots into the oil and fry for about 5 minutes, by which time they should have turned a dark golden brown. Transfer to a piece of kitchen roll to drain off any excess oil (give them a light press to remove as much oil as you can). Season with a little salt and keep to one side.

In a bowl mix together the oyster sauce and soy sauce with the remaining shaosing.

Heat the remaining rice bran oil in your wok over a high heat. Once hot, add the mushrooms and stir-fry for 1 minute. Then add the garlic and spring onions. Continue to stir-fry for a further minute before reducing the heat and piling in the pea shoots along with the oyster sauce mixture and 2 tablespoons of water. Don't worry if it seems like the pea shoots won't all fit; they will quickly wilt. Give them a stir and when they have wilted, remove from the heat.

To serve, cover the base of a large serving dish with the pea shoot mixture. Carefully remove the fish from its parcel and place on top. Drizzle any of the cooking liquid over the fish and finish with a final flurry of the fried shallots. Perfect dinner party food to serve to your nearest and dearest.

267
CALORIES
6.6g
FAT
1g
SAT FAT
4.6g
SUGAR
2.2g
SALT

10-MINUTE NOODLES

Amidst our hectic modern lives, it is easy to put a dinner date in the diary and then completely forget about it until an hour before your guests are due to arrive. With nothing in the fridge apart from half a bottle of wine, you begin wondering how you can dress up a takeaway as a home-cooked meal. Well, fear not, as here is a recipe that delivers maximum flavour using only long-lasting store-cupboard basics and which will be ready in under half an hour.

SERVES 4

2 tbsp rice bran oil or vegetable oil

300g frozen prawns

1 red onion, peeled and roughly sliced into thin wedges

4 cloves of garlic, peeled and finely chopped

a 3cm piece of fresh ginger, peeled and finely diced

2 fresh red chillies, deseeded and finely sliced (leave in the seeds if you prefer it hotter)

80g frozen broad beans

80g frozen peas

80g drained water chestnuts, roughly chopped

350g straight-to-wok thick udon noodles

1 tbsp light soy sauce

1 tbsp dark soy sauce

2 tsp fish sauce

lime juice, to serve

optional: sweet chilli sauce, to serve

Heat half of the oil in a wok over a medium to high heat. When hot, add the prawns and fry for 2–3 minutes, stirring every now and then, until they have defrosted and turned a delicious coral colour (they won't be fully cooked at this point). Tip the prawns on to a plate and wipe your wok clean with kitchen roll.

Heat the remaining oil in the wok over a medium to high heat. Once hot, fry the onion for 1 minute before adding the garlic, ginger and chillies. Stir-fry for a further minute and then return the half-cooked prawns to the wok. Heat through for 1–2 minutes and then add the beans and peas. Stir-fry the whole lot for a further 2–3 minutes until everything is heated through.

Add the remaining ingredients apart from the lime juice and sweet chilli sauce and toss together until well combined. Don't even mess around plating up this dish, just place the wok in the middle of the table with the lime wedges and chilli sauce, if using, alongside and revel in the eating-induced silence that is sure to fall over your friends.

346
CALORIES

7.1g
FAT

1.4g
SAT FAT

2.7g
SUGAR

3g
SALT

STEAMED LOBSTER IN LOTUS LEAF

This is the Coco Chanel of the dinner-party scene. As sophisticated and as elegant as any dish in the world, this is one that should only be pulled out on the most special of occasions, and only for those most important to you. Lotus leaves aren't difficult to find in your local Asian supermarket, but you could use tin foil if you really have to. And make sure you find yourself a respectable fishmonger who treats his lobsters humanely. They are out there.

SERVES 4

2 x 800g raw lobster, dispatched
    humanely

1 tbsp light soy sauce

1 tbsp shaosing or dry sherry

1 large lotus leaf, soaked in cold water
    for 30 minutes

a 4cm piece of fresh ginger, peeled
    and sliced into long matchsticks

2 fresh red chillies, deseeded and
    finely sliced

4 spring onions, trimmed and finely
    sliced on an angle

400g cooked jasmine rice

2 x quantities of red chilli and anchovy
    broccoli, to serve (see page 190)

Prepare the lobster by first pulling off the claws. Use the back of a heavy knife or a meat hammer to crack some of the shell on the claws so that the heat will be able to get through and cook the flesh. Holding the body of the lobster in two hands, pull the head away from the main tail. The head can now be discarded, or cleaned out and cooked with the rest for decoration.

Place the tail flat on a chopping board (lay a tea towel underneath the chopping board to keep it steady). Using a sharp knife cut the lobster straight through the shell into 4 large chunks. Place the claws and the chopped pieces of tail in a bowl. Pour over the soy sauce and shaosing and leave to rest for 5 minutes to let the flavours work into the flesh.

Cut the stalk from the middle of the soaked lotus leaf and line a medium-sized steamer basket with the leaf. (It may not be necessary to use the whole leaf, and there may be a fair amount of cutting and folding. Don't worry about it being too neat!)

When the steamer basket is lined, tip the lobster pieces along with the liquids into the leaf. Scatter over the ginger. Place the lid on top and then position the basket over a wok filled with boiling water over a medium heat (making sure the water doesn't touch the bottom of the steamer). Let the lobster steam for about 20 minutes, until the flesh has turned a deep coral colour, is firm to the touch and is starting to pull away from the shell.

Once it's ready, remove the lid, and scatter over the chillies and spring onion. Serve the steamer basket in the middle of the table (over a bowl or serving dish to catch any drips) alongside the jasmine rice and broccoli.

DATE NIGHT

I love dating. I'm a self-confessed dateaholic. There's nothing I love more than a six-hour flirtathon: shy smiles, prolonged eye contact and a strategic extra opened button. But what really excites me is creating the ambiance. How many candles to light? Which music to play? What should I wear? And, of course, what food should I serve?

I'm a firm believer that certain foods go with certain stages of dating. For instance, a first-base date needs to be simple, elegant and, above all, easy to eat – something uncomplicated. You don't want the food to upstage the conversation, as it's you that has to shine. The second-base date should be more intriguing – you have to make him or her want you. Serving something that is a little unexpected will absolutely leave them wanting more. The third-base date needs to be more confirmed; it's about bagging your prize and making your date believe that they couldn't spend another second without you. It's vital you serve something they've never tried before – you are unique! And the fourth-base date is like marriage food: it's about sharing a dish and experiencing a place neither of you have been to before, after all you are nesting for the future.

There is nothing more attractive than confidence. I know that dating can be scary, so ensure you feel confident with your menu and then you'll have more energy to concentrate on your date.

SALMON AND CUCUMBER SASHIMI

Make sure you use the freshest salmon you can find for this recipe, as you will be eating the fish when it is raw. This is ridiculously tasty served on top of a rice cake with a dash of mirin, but for a more filling option you could serve it mixed through some steamed brown rice. Although quite high in calories, this dish is packed with healthy fats from the salmon and avocado.

SERVES 2

1 spring onion, trimmed and very finely sliced

175g very fresh salmon fillet, skin removed, chopped into 0.5cm dice

2 tsp light soy sauce

½ tsp sesame oil

½ a cucumber, peeled, halved lengthways and deseeded, chopped into 0.5cm dice

½ tsp sugar

1 tbsp rice wine vinegar

6 rice cakes, to serve

1 avocado, stone removed, peeled and sliced, to serve

Place the spring onion, salmon, soy sauce and sesame oil in a bowl. Mix well and leave to one side while you pickle the cucumber.

Place the cucumber, sugar and vinegar in a shallow bowl and mix until well combined.

Leave the salmon and the cucumber to one side for 10 minutes. Don't leave them any longer, as the salmon will start to 'cook' in the soy sauce and the cucumber will lose its crunch.

After 10 minutes, drain the cucumber of its pickling liquid. Add the cucumber to the marinated salmon and mix together.

Spoon generously on top of the rice cakes, topped with slices of avocado. Alternatively, crumble the rice cakes and serve alongside the sashimi and avocado.

30
CALORIES

0.4g
FAT

0.1g
SAT FAT

0.2g
SUGAR

0.7g
SALT

PRAWN AND WATERCRESS DUMPLINGS

When I filmed *Gok Cooks Chinese* I had the great pleasure of meeting a dynamic mother-daughter cooking duo running a tiny dumpling kitchen in the heart of Brixton market. Their menu is so small it could be written on a post-it note, but every dish is delicious. It was there that I learned how to cook these little healthy parcels of joy and happiness. Although I had made dumplings before, I had never made water dumplings . . . mine had always been partly fried. These are super-healthy, as they are dropped into boiling water and cooked in minutes with NO oil. What could be easier? I have tried many fillings, but watercress and prawn is by far my favourite: light and flavoursome, and so satisfying I often make a plate of them for my supper, sharing with no one . . . not even the dog!

MAKES 8

9 raw king prawns, shelled, de-veined and chopped fairly finely
1 tsp chopped fresh chives
½ tsp sesame oil
½ tsp light soy sauce, plus extra to serve
15g watercress, finely chopped
8 ready-made wonton wrappers
salt and white pepper
optional: soy sauce, to serve

Place all of the ingredients apart from the wonton wrappers in a bowl. Season with a little salt and pepper, then mix well to combine.

Take one of the wonton wrappers and place a generously heaped teaspoon of the mixture in the centre. Using your finger, brush a little water around the edge of the wrapper. Now you need to seal your dumpling. Hold the wonton flat in the palm of your hand and, using your other hand, draw the closest and furthest edges together and pinch them so that they stick. Carefully seal the remaining edges together, trying to avoid trapping any air in the wonton. If you're feeling fancy, you can pleat the sealed edge, but it's not essential. Place your finished wonton to one side, and repeat with the rest of the wonton wrappers and the filling.

When all your dumplings are ready, bring a saucepan of water to the boil and carefully drop them in. Gently boil for 4–6 minutes, until the wonton wrappers turn slightly translucent and are soft to the touch. Drain and serve, with a little soy sauce to dip if you like.

SUMMER ROLLS

153
CALORIES
3.6g
FAT
0.6g
SAT FAT
2.5g
SUGAR
1.6g
SALT

These are the most deliciously refreshing morsels to come out of Vietnam. They taste good for you, and they are. Perfect date food, but so moreish and easy to make that they can be eaten at any time – even pack a couple for lunch. So, if and when you feel the need to realign your dietary karma, prepare this recipe for guilt-free eating that is full of flavour.

MAKES 6

juice of 2 limes

1 tbsp fish sauce

2 tsp sugar

1 clove of garlic, peeled and minced or grated

¼ of an iceberg lettuce, shredded

2 tbsp fresh Thai basil, shredded

2 tbsp fresh mint, shredded

2 tbsp fresh coriander, shredded

40g raw peanuts, roughly chopped

1 fresh red chilli, finely chopped

1 tbsp rice bran oil or vegetable oil

6 dried summer roll wrappers, about 15cm in diameter

18 cooked and peeled, medium-sized prawns

250g cooked and cooled vermicelli noodles

4 tbsp sweet chilli sauce, to serve

Put the lime juice, fish sauce, sugar and garlic in a small bowl. Add 3 tablespoons of water and mix well until the sugar has completely dissolved.

Place the shredded lettuce, basil, mint, coriander, peanuts and chilli in a separate bowl. Pour over the dressing and toss together until all the ingredients are lightly coated.

Fill a small bowl with warm tap water. Lightly oil a small space of work surface or a chopping board. Dip one of the wrappers in the water and pull it out almost immediately. Lay the wrapper on the oiled surface. Lay 3 prawns in the middle of the wrapper, from left to right, leaving a wide edge all the way round. Place some of the cooked noodles and dressed salad on top.

Fold both ends of the wrapper over the filling and then lift the edge closest to you, folding it over the filling. Roll the whole thing over, away from you, so that all the edges are enclosed.

Repeat with the remaining wrappers and ingredients. Serve your delicious rolls with sweet chilli dipping sauce.

126
CALORIES

9.3g
FAT

1.8g
SAT FAT

2.7g
SUGAR

1.7g
SALT

SCALLOPS WITH CUCUMBER AND TOMATO RELISH

Will he touch my hand as he reaches for his glass? The way his lip curls at the edge when he gets nervous drives me crazy with excitement. How long before he kisses me? I love dating! There, I said it . . . Sue me or buy me another drink. I don't care which; just let me flirt a little while longer!

SERVES 2

2 tbsp rice wine vinegar

1 tsp sugar

¼ of a cucumber, peeled, halved lengthways and deseeded, diced into 0.5cm pieces

2 tbsp rice bran oil or vegetable oil

1 fresh red chilli, deseeded and finely chopped

1 clove of garlic, peeled and finely chopped

3 tinned anchovy fillets, drained and finely chopped

1 tbsp dark soy sauce

6 scallops, coral removed and cleaned

1 tomato, deseeded and chopped into 0.5cm dice

1 spring onion, trimmed and finely sliced

salt and white pepper

25g pea shoots, to serve

Start by mixing together the vinegar, sugar and 1 teaspoon of salt. Add the cucumber, stir a couple of times and leave to pickle for about 10 minutes.

In the meantime, heat half the oil in a wok over a medium to high heat. When hot, add the chilli, garlic and anchovies. Stir-fry for 1 minute and then add 2 tablespoons of water and the soy sauce. Continue cooking for a further 2 minutes or until the liquid has reduced by half, then remove from the heat and keep to one side.

Heat the remaining oil in a clean frying pan or wok over a high heat. Season the scallops with salt and pepper. When the oil is hot, fry the scallops for about 2 minutes on each side. They are cooked when they are golden brown and the flesh is firm but still has a little bounce to it. Remove from the pan and let the scallops rest for a couple of minutes.

Drain the cucumber of its pickling liquid and toss together with the tomato and spring onion.

To serve, spoon the relish on to a large plate. Top with the scallops, drizzle with the anchovy sauce and finish with a flourish of pea shoots.

319
CALORIES

11.9g
FAT

4.4g
SAT FAT

2.8g
SUGAR

1.3g
SALT

FIVE-SPICE STEAK AND HERB SALAD

When you're on a date and want to win over his heart, serve him a steak and he'll definitely come back for more. But what he won't be expecting are the surprise spices in this recipe. The marinade uses one of the most traditional flavours in Asian cuisine and one that you won't find anywhere else in the world. And using Chinese five spice is really easy, as all the work's done for you! Date night just got spicy.

SERVES 2

1 tbsp hoisin sauce

½ tsp Chinese five spice

2 x 200g trimmed sirloin steak

½ tbsp sesame oil

2 tbsp rice wine vinegar

1 tsp agave nectar or palm sugar

3 tbsp celery leaves

3 tbsp fresh parsley leaves

2 tbsp chives, roughly chopped

2 tbsp fresh mint leaves

salt and white pepper

Mix together the hoisin sauce, five spice and a generous amount of white pepper until well combined.

Spread a large piece of cling film over a chopping board. Place the trimmed steaks on top and cover with another large piece of cling film. Using a meat hammer or a rolling pin, bash the steaks until they are half the thickness and twice the size. Place your flattened meat in a shallow dish and smother it with the hoisin sauce marinade. Leave the steak to marinate for at least 30 minutes, but no more than overnight.

When ready to cook, heat a griddle pan over a high heat. When the pan is scorching hot carefully lay the steaks on to cook. For medium-rare, fry the steaks for 1 minute on each side, and then transfer to a board and leave to rest for 5 minutes. (If you prefer your steaks well done then fry them for a minute or two longer, but do not skip the resting time, as this is what gives your steaks a meltingly tender texture.)

While your steaks are resting, mix together the sesame oil and the vinegar. Place all of the herb leaves in a bowl and pour over the dressing. Mix well, adding a sprinkle of salt and pepper.

Serve the steaks with the herb salad.

 TIP: Serve this with the sweet potato chips on page 189 for an Asian take on classic steak and chips.

327
CALORIES

17.8g
FAT

6.9g
SAT FAT

17g
SUGAR

2.1g
SALT

STICKY RIBS

Ribs don't seem like the obvious choice for a date night, but that's because you're not thinking of them in the correct light. Let me paint you a picture: sticky ribs picked up with delicate fingers, the tender meat gently teased from the bone . . . Now do you see what I mean? I concede, this may not be a dish for the first date, but from the third date on, these ribs will have anybody swooning into your freshly wet-wiped arms.

SERVES 2

800g pork spare ribs

250ml shaosing or dry sherry

100ml light soy sauce, plus 1 tbsp

2 star anise

a 5cm piece of fresh ginger, peeled and roughly sliced

4 cloves of garlic, peeled and bashed

1 onion, peeled and roughly chopped

3 tbsp clear honey

Place the ribs in a large saucepan. Pour in the shaosing, the 100ml of soy sauce and enough water to cover the ribs. Gently mix in the star anise, ginger, garlic and onion. Bring to the boil over a medium heat, then reduce the heat and simmer for 40 minutes. Remove from the heat and leave to cool to room temperature. Once cooled, remove the ribs, pat them dry with kitchen roll and separate into individual ribs. Discard the cooking liquid.

Preheat your oven to 200°C/400°F/Gas mark 6. Line a large baking tray with foil. Mix together the honey and the remaining tablespoon of soy sauce. Coat the ribs in the honey mixture and arrange them on the baking tray.

Roast the ribs for about 20–30 minutes, turning and basting them a couple of times. They are ready when they have turned a dark golden colour.

Serve to your date, and if they don't like them, show them the door!

230
CALORIES
9.9g
FAT
1.5g
SAT FAT
2.1g
SUGAR
1.3g
SALT

STEAMED SEA BASS PARCELS

Everyone loves a present, especially on a date. This dish truly is a culinary gift with everything steamed and served in the same foil parcel. It is packed full of fresh ingredients that are light and super tasty, but the real beauty lies in the fact that there's no washing up needed . . . more time for snogging.

SERVES 2

100g Tenderstem broccoli, trimmed

½ tbsp sesame oil

2 x 120g sea bass fillets, bones removed

a 2cm piece of fresh ginger, peeled and chopped into matchsticks

6 raw queen scallops

4 oyster mushrooms, torn into rough pieces

2 spring onions, trimmed and finely chopped

2 tsp soy sauce

2 tbsp shaosing or dry sherry

white pepper

Bring a saucepan of water to the boil over a medium heat and blanch the broccoli for 2–3 minutes. Refresh in cold water and set aside. Preheat the oven to 200°C/400°F/Gas mark 6.

Make the fish parcels one at a time. Take a 60cm piece of foil and fold it in half so you have a 30cm piece at double thickness. With the shorter side facing you, drizzle a little sesame oil in the middle of the foil. Place the fish fillet, flesh-side down, on top of the oil. Scatter over half the ginger and arrange half the scallops, oyster mushrooms, spring onions and broccoli on top. Season with half the soy sauce, and a generous amount of white pepper.

Bring the foil edge that is furthest from you over the top of the fish until it meets the edge closest to you; fold together to seal. Seal one of the remaining open sides. Drizzle half of the shaosing into the remaining open side before sealing and placing the whole package on a baking tray. Repeat the process with the rest of the ingredients.

Cook in the oven for 10 minutes. Remove from the oven and leave the fish to sit for a further minute, before carefully tearing open the packages.

 TIP: Watch your fingers when opening the packages, as the steam will be very hot.

GRILLED PORK CHOP WITH CIDER SALSA

483
CALORIES
10.6g
FAT
3.3g
SAT FAT
22.3g
SUGAR
1.8g
SALT

The sun is shining, there's a warm breeze in the air and your new 'friend' is coming over for dinner. You want something that is fun, delicious and just that little bit flirtatious and this dish is all that and more.

SERVES 2

200ml cider

2 x 250g trimmed pork chops on the bone

2 tsp fish sauce

juice of ½ a lime

1 fresh red chilli, deseeded and finely sliced

1 tomato, deseeded and finely sliced

1 mango, peeled and chopped into small dice

1 small red onion, peeled and finely sliced

salt and white pepper

1 baked sweet potato, to serve

Preheat your grill as hot as it gets. Pour the cider into a saucepan and bring to the boil over a medium heat. Simmer until it has reduced by three-quarters.

While the cider is reducing, season the pork chops with a little salt and pepper. Place them under the grill and cook for about 5 minutes on each side, until lightly browned and cooked all the way through.

When the cider has reduced stir in the fish sauce and lime juice.

Mix together the remaining ingredients in a small bowl, and then pour over the cider dressing. Serve the grilled pork chops topped with tangy salsa, and half a baked potato each.

371
CALORIES
7.9g
FAT
1.9g
SAT FAT
6.8g
SUGAR
1.8g
SALT

SWEET MISO MARINATED CHICKEN AND PAK CHOY

Knowing what to cook on a date is an art form. It's all about enticing, and showing off your best assets. This dish will show you off as the perfect evening companion, full of flavour, beautiful to look at and a total one-off. But while you're looking into his eyes, don't be unfaithful to your taste buds.

SERVES 4

4 heads of pak choy

250ml miso stock

4 spring onions, trimmed and finely sliced

a 2cm piece of fresh ginger, peeled and finely diced

2 cloves of garlic, peeled and finely diced

2 tbsp agave nectar or honey

1 tbsp light soy sauce

1 tbsp dark soy sauce

8 x 80g skinless, boneless chicken thighs

400g steamed rice, to serve

Bring a saucepan of water to the boil over a medium heat and blanch the pak choy for 3–4 minutes. Refresh in cold water, halve them lengthways and set aside.

Place the miso, spring onions, ginger and garlic in a saucepan. Bring to the boil over a high heat and cook until reduced by half. Stir in the agave nectar and both of the soy sauces. Pour the miso mixture over the chicken and leave to marinate in the fridge for at least 20 minutes, or ideally overnight.

Preheat the grill as high as it will go and line your grill tray with foil. Lay the chicken thighs in a single layer on the foil and place under the hot grill. Cook for 8–10 minutes, by which time the chicken should have begun to colour.

Turn the chicken thighs over and add the pak choy to the tray, dotted between the chicken. Cook for 5–6 minutes, until the chicken is firm to the touch, which means it is cooked through (check that there is no pink meat inside, if you're not sure), and the pak choy is warmed through and a little charred.

Remove the tray from the oven and serve this easy one-tray dish with steamed rice.

770
CALORIES

34.8g
FAT

7.2g
SAT FAT

4.5g
SUGAR

2.8g
SALT

TUNA WRAPPED IN CORIANDER WITH PICKLED MUSHROOMS

Date night should be about treating yourself. Armed with this sophisticated and stunningly beautiful dish, your date will have no choice but to fall madly in love with you. Just be sure to buy the best-quality tuna you can find, as you will be eating it almost totally raw.

SERVES 2

500ml rice wine vinegar

1 tsp coriander seeds

1 tbsp sugar

1 tbsp salt

1 bay leaf

2 red bird's eye chillies, split lengthways

400g mixed mushrooms, wiped clean and cut to similar sizes

1 x 350g very fresh tuna steak

3 tbsp chopped fresh coriander

2 tbsp black sesame seeds

1 tbsp rice bran oil or vegetable oil

1 avocado, stone removed, peeled and chopped

salt and white pepper

½ x quantity of sushi rice, to serve (see page 204)

Begin by pickling the mushrooms. This process has to start at least 3 hours before you want to serve dinner. (They work very well if you make them the night before, and leave them in the fridge overnight.) Place the vinegar, coriander seeds, sugar, salt, bay leaf and chillies in a large saucepan. Bring to the boil over a medium heat and stir until the sugar and salt have dissolved.

Remove the pan from the heat and drop in all of the mushrooms. They may not all submerge in the liquid, but don't worry. Let the mushrooms sit in the pickling liquor for a minimum of 3 hours, turning them every now and then.

When ready to eat, drain the mushrooms through a sieve and discard all the flavourings.

Trim the tuna so you are left with an almost perfect square. (Keep the trimmings in the fridge to use in another meal like the egg not-so fried rice on page 28.) Slice the tuna in half through the middle, and wrap each piece tightly in cling film to create an even square shape (you may need to mould it slightly with your hands). Leave the wrapped tuna in the fridge for a minimum of 15 minutes, but this also can be prepared and left overnight.

When ready to cook, tip the chopped coriander and the sesame seeds on to a plate along with a little salt and a pinch of white pepper. Unwrap the shaped tuna steaks and coat them in the coriander and sesame seed mix.

Heat the oil in a frying pan over a high heat. When very hot, gently lay the tuna pieces in the oil. Cook for 40 seconds, rolling the tuna so it cooks all over, then transfer to a plate. Let the tuna rest for 1 minute before slicing into 1cm-thick rounds.

Serve the sliced tuna with the pickled mushrooms, avocado pieces and the rice.

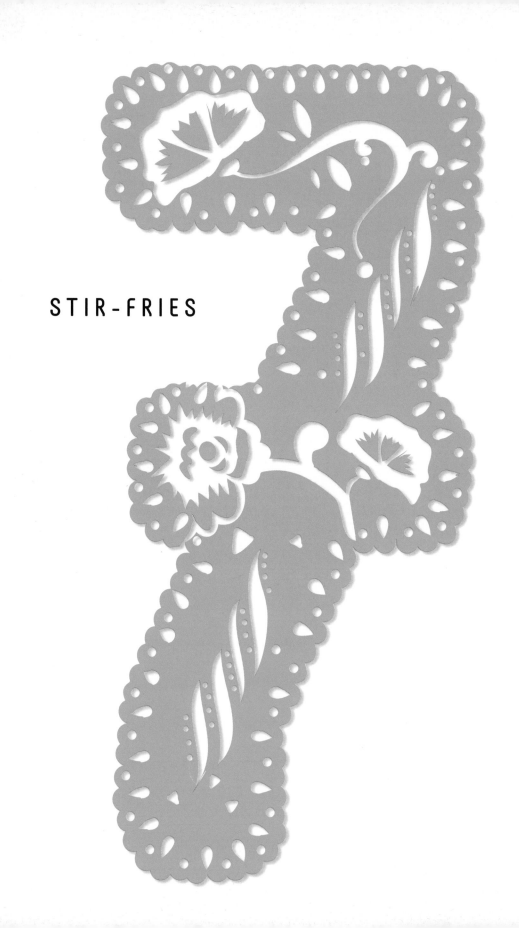

STIR-FRIES

Stir-fries are as Asian as longboats and emperors and they are also the perfect food for your hectic schedule. I get it, it's 7 p.m., your feet feel like they've been bound, you're wearing 12-hour mascara, one kid is strapped to the other kid's head and the last thing you want to do is cook a family meal. What do you do? Reach for a bag of frozen whatever or heat up a pot of cream and cheese sauce and chuck it over some pasta? Do you need any more guilt in your life? Well, fear not, Auntie Gok and his virtuous wok are coming to the rescue!

Stir-frying is quick, simple and has health benefits that would make even the Dalai Lama blush. Because of the quick frying in minimal oil, the ingredients retain all their vitamins and minerals, giving your family a nutritional boost. It's also an incredible way of using up whatever you've got in the fridge the day before you go food shopping. And, because you only need one piece of cooking equipment, washing up is reduced to a mere rinse. Busy people, stir-fry your way to an easy life. May the wok be with you!

I am impatient by nature and I ain't wasting no time cooking when I've a drink in my hand and there's a laugh to be had. Stir-frying is shamefully easy and exactly what is says on the tin. You can throw in any ingredients you have in your store and fridge, but the one thing you must remember is that seasoning is king.

474
CALORIES
11.6g
FAT
2.5g
SAT FAT
7.3g
SUGAR
2g
SALT

SINGAPORE VERMICELLI

This is a super-speedy stir-fry made with fresh and crunchy ingredients – it's a wonderful combination of tastes and textures. When we worked in the restaurant, this was a staff dinner either before or after service. Dad would cook up a massive wok of rice and, as soon as I walked in the door and I could smell it from the front counter, it would make me so happy that I would skip to the back of the kitchen where we would all eat together.

SERVES 2

350g skinless, boneless chicken thighs, chopped into bite-sized pieces

2 tbsp curry powder

1 tbsp rice bran oil or vegetable oil

1 small red onion, peeled and sliced

2 cloves of garlic, peeled and finely sliced

1 carrot, peeled and chopped into 0.5cm slices on the diagonal

1 stick of celery, chopped into 0.5cm slices on the diagonal

a large handful of mange tout (approx. 150g)

300g soaked and cooled vermicelli noodles

1 tbsp soy sauce

white pepper

Place the chicken in a bowl and scatter over half of the curry powder. Add a little white pepper and mix well so that all of the chicken is coated with the seasoning. Leave to sit at room temperature for 5 minutes.

Heat the oil in a wok over a high heat. Once hot, add the chicken pieces and fry for 3–4 minutes, turning a couple of times, until almost cooked through. Add the onion, garlic, carrot and celery. Stir-fry for 2–3 minutes and then sprinkle over the remaining curry powder. Continue to stir-fry for a further minute or so before mixing in the mange tout.

Drop the noodles into the wok, add the soy sauce and mix thoroughly until warmed through.

442
CALORIES
12.8g
FAT
4g
SAT FAT
5.4g
SUGAR
1.9g
SALT

BEEF, SWEET PEA AND BLACK BEANS

The Chinese staple menu consists of just a handful of sauces, with oyster, yellow bean and black bean being the most popular. Black bean is my favourite. It's a wonderfully deep sauce filled with layer upon layer of flavour. In this recipe, the bitterness of the black beans works harmoniously with a single fiery chilli. Add whatever vegetables you like but sweet garden peas are a beautiful companion for the beef; they sit elegantly together, neither one wanting to upstage the other.

SERVES 4

2 tbsp rice bran oil or vegetable oil

500g trimmed sirloin steak, sliced into 1cm strips

4 cloves of garlic, peeled and finely chopped

a 2cm piece of fresh ginger, peeled and finely chopped

1 bird's eye chilli, finely chopped (seeds removed if you don't like it too hot)

1 red onion, peeled and roughly sliced

1 red pepper, deseeded and chopped into 0.5cm slices

1 tbsp black beans, soaked in warm water for 20 minutes

200g frozen peas

2 tbsp oyster sauce

1 tbsp soy sauce

white pepper

400g steamed rice, to serve

100g pea shoots, to serve

Heat the oil in a wok over a high heat. Season the beef strips with pepper. When the oil is hot, stir-fry the beef for 30 seconds until the meat has browned all over.

Add the garlic, ginger, chilli, onion and pepper. Stir-fry for a further 2 minutes before adding the black beans and peas. Stir-fry for 1–2 minutes, until the peas are warmed through. Pour in the oyster and soy sauces and mix well to combine.

Serve this effortlessly delicious stir-fry alongside freshly steamed rice and topped with pea shoots.

629 CALORIES
20.8g FAT
5.7g SAT FAT
5.5g SUGAR
2.2g SALT

CHILLI BEEF AND LONG BEAN

One of the greatest gifts Poppa Wan gave me was the gift of stir-fry. He watched over me as I filled my wok with carefully chopped ingredients and mentored me until I got it right. If you master the skill of throwing everything into a hot wok, and seasoning it just right, I guarantee it will change the way you cook for the rest of your life. It did me.

SERVES 4

2 tbsp rice bran oil or vegetable oil

400g sirloin steaks, trimmed and sliced into 1cm strips

300g green beans, topped, tail left on

4 spring onions, trimmed, halved and bashed

2 cloves of garlic, peeled and roughly chopped

2 fresh red chillies, deseeded and finely sliced (leave the seeds in if you like it hotter)

1 tsp dried chilli flakes

6 water chestnuts, drained and roughly chopped

100g bean sprouts

1½ tbsp light soy sauce

1 tsp fish sauce

salt and white pepper

400g egg noodles, cooked according to packet instructions, dressed with 2 tsp sesame oil, to serve

Heat half of the oil in a wok over a high heat. Season the steak with salt and pepper. Once the oil is hot, stir-fry the beef for 2 minutes, then transfer to a plate.

Wipe your wok clean with some kitchen roll and heat the remaining oil over a high heat. Once hot, add the green beans and stir-fry for 2 minutes, until they are lightly blistered and dark golden in places.

Carefully pour in 2 tablespoons of water – it will hiss and spit and almost instantly evaporate. Reduce the heat a little and add the spring onions, garlic and fresh chillies. Continue to stir-fry for 1 minute.

Add the dried chilli flakes along with the water chestnuts, bean sprouts and browned beef. Stir-fry for 2 minutes, then pour in the soy sauce and the fish sauce. Season with a little pepper. Stir-fry until all the ingredients are well mixed and heated through.

Serve the fiery beef with warm egg noodles for a comforting mid-week meal.

381
CALORIES

13.3g
FAT

2.7g
SAT FAT

4.1g
SUGAR

1g
SALT

XO STIR-FRY

XO stir-fry represents premier Hong Kong Chinese cooking. The traditional XO sauce is made from scratch using dried scallops and Chinese ham, but, luckily, you can now buy it in a bottle from your local Asian supermarket. If you don't have the budget or the appetite for shellfish, then you can make this with thin strips of chicken (they will take a bit longer to cook).

SERVES 2

200g Tenderstem broccoli, trimmed

3 tsp rice bran oil or vegetable oil

6 scallops, cleaned, roe removed and
    sliced into half-moons

1 rasher of smoked, streaky bacon,
    sliced into 1cm strips

a 2cm piece of fresh ginger, peeled
    and finely sliced

1 clove of garlic, peeled and finely
    sliced

2 spring onions, trimmed and chopped
    into 1cm pieces

1 fresh red chilli, deseeded and finely
    diced

1 tbsp XO sauce

salt and white pepper

¼ of an iceberg lettuce, shredded,
    to serve

300g cooked jasmine rice, to serve

Bring a saucepan of water to the boil and blanch the broccoli for 3 minutes. Drain and cool under cold water. Set aside.

Heat half of the oil in a wok over a high heat. Season the scallops with salt and pepper. Once the oil is hot, add the scallops and fry for about a minute on each side, until they are lightly browned and almost cooked through. Tip the scallops on to a plate.

Wipe out the wok with some kitchen roll, pour in the remaining oil and heat over a medium to high heat. Stir-fry the bacon for 30 seconds before adding the ginger, garlic and spring onions. Continue to stir-fry for 2 minutes. Tumble in the blanched broccoli, the chilli and the partially cooked scallops and stir-fry for 2 minutes, then pour in the XO sauce. Turn off the heat and toss all the ingredients together so that they are coated in the sauce. Serve with crunchy iceberg lettuce and cooked rice.

370 CALORIES
13.5g FAT
3.2g SAT FAT
4.7g SUGAR
4.5g SALT

MIXED SEAFOOD NASI GORENG

There are certain meals that you eat on holiday that taste so good you end up eating them for breakfast, lunch and dinner. Nasi goreng is one of those dishes. If you've ever been lucky enough to visit Indonesia, then you will have surely eaten several plates of this delicious rice meal. You may not be able to afford to travel back to Indonesia for another taste, but this recipe will remind you of sunnier times.

SERVES 4

3 eggs

2 tbsp light soy sauce

1 tsp sesame oil

2 tbsp rice bran oil or vegetable oil

3 cloves of garlic, peeled and finely diced

a 3cm piece of fresh ginger, peeled and finely diced

1 onion, peeled and finely diced

3 tinned anchovy fillets, drained and roughly chopped

400g mixed, cooked seafood (a mixture of squid, mussels and prawns)

400g cooked and cooled long grain rice

3 tbsp Ketcap Manis

2 tsp fish sauce

a small salad of sliced cucumber, shredded iceberg lettuce and sliced tomatoes, to serve

lemon wedges, to serve

Crack the eggs into a bowl and pour in 1 tablespoon of the light soy sauce and all of the sesame oil. Heat half of the rice bran oil in a wok over a high heat. When hot, pour in the egg and let it set for about 30 seconds before breaking it up with your spoon and stir-frying for a further 2 minutes. You are aiming for large pieces of lightly browned egg. Tip the egg on to a plate while you cook the rest of the ingredients.

Wipe out the wok with some kitchen roll, add the rest of the oil and place it back over a medium to high heat. Once hot, add the garlic, ginger, onion and anchovies. Stir-fry for 2–3 minutes before tipping in the mixed seafood. Toss the ingredients together so that they are well mixed.

Add the cooked and cooled rice to the wok and break it up with a spoon. Pour in the Ketcap Manis, the fish sauce and the remaining soy sauce. Continue to stir-fry for a further minute.

Pile on to plates and serve with the salad and a lemon wedge.

181	CALORIES
8.1g	FAT
1.4g	SAT FAT
1.5g	SUGAR
2.3g	SALT

VIRGIN MUSHROOM STIR-FRY

We all know that stir-fries are über healthy, but even the most careful of chefs can sometimes be guilty of adding too many sauces and salts. I want you to trust what you taste and only add as much or as little flavouring as you feel is really necessary. Top tip: Coco Chanel once advised us to remove at least one accessory before leaving the house. I've used this principle in this dish.

SERVES 4

1 tbsp rice bran oil or vegetable oil

2 cloves of garlic, peeled and finely chopped

a 3cm piece of fresh ginger, peeled and finely chopped

2 large sticks of celery, sliced diagonally into 1cm slices

4 spring onions, trimmed, halved and bashed

450g mixed exotic mushrooms (such as oyster, shimeji or shiitake – you can even used dried mushrooms, rehydrated), roughly chopped

10 bamboo shoots

2 tbsp oyster sauce

1 tbsp light soy sauce

1 tbsp fish sauce

4 tbsp pumpkin seeds

white pepper

400g cooked egg noodles, to serve

Heat the oil in a wok over a high heat. When hot, add the garlic, ginger, celery and spring onions and stir-fry for 2 minutes. Add all of the mushrooms and continue to stir-fry for about 4 minutes, until the mushrooms begin to wilt and take on a little colour. Add the bamboo shoots and stir to combine.

Pour in the oyster, soy and fish sauces along with a good pinch of white pepper. Stir-fry for a further minute to warm through and then scatter over the pumpkin seeds and serve with the egg noodles.

 Tip: Never, ever wash your mushrooms. If you really need to clean them, wipe them gently with a damp cloth.

291
CALORIES
12g
FAT
1.8g
SAT FAT
5.9g
SUGAR
1.8g
SALT

AUBERGINE AND SHIITAKE MUSHROOM

There's something satisfyingly hearty about aubergines and mushrooms that will convince even the most ardent of carnivores that you can have a complete meal without a chunk of meat. To make this dish into a full veggie dish, simply drop the anchovies and add a little extra soy sauce.

SERVES 4

3 tbsp rice bran oil or vegetable oil

1 aubergine, chopped into rough 2cm chunks

4 tinned anchovy fillets, drained and roughly chopped

1 large onion, peeled and sliced into thin wedges

4 cloves of garlic, peeled and finely chopped

200g fresh shiitake mushrooms, cleaned and roughly chopped in half

2 tbsp shaosing or dry sherry

450g straight-to-wok udon noodles, rinsed in hot water

1 tbsp light soy sauce

1 tbsp dark soy sauce

1 tbsp toasted sesame oil

4 spring onions, trimmed and chopped into 1cm pieces

2 fresh red chillies, deseeded and finely sliced (leave the seeds in if you like it hotter)

Heat half of the oil in a wok over a high heat. When hot, tip in the diced aubergine and fry for 2–3 minutes, stirring occasionally, until most of the pieces have taken on a golden colour. Transfer the cooked aubergine to a plate.

Wipe out the wok with some kitchen roll, add the remaining oil and heat over a medium to high heat. Once hot, add the anchovies, onion and garlic. Stir-fry for about 3 minutes, until the onions are starting to soften, then add the mushrooms and the aubergine pieces. Pour in the shaosing and let it bubble up and almost totally evaporate. Add a couple of tablespoons of water to help the mushrooms cook a little. Once the water has evaporated, tumble in the noodles and toss together with the rest of the ingredients.

Pour in both the soy sauces and the sesame oil and mix to combine. Remove the wok from the heat and scatter over the spring onions and chillies. Don't even bother plating this one up, just place it in the centre of the table with a load of chopsticks and watch the gastronomic carnage unfold.

200
CALORIES

7.8g
FAT

1.4g
SAT FAT

1.6g
SUGAR

2.2g
SALT

PRAWN AND LITTLE GEM

The Chinese have been cooking lettuce for as long as they've been flying kites. Dad would often serve lettuce with oyster sauce in the restaurant and it is one of my favourite dishes. I've used prawns in my version and, to create a more rounded meal, I've added noodles. This is a very simple dish and I promise you that whomever you serve it to will imagine you've been cooking for years.

SERVES 4

2 tbsp rice bran oil or vegetable oil

350g raw king prawns, shelled

3 spring onions, trimmed and chopped into 1cm pieces

3 cloves of garlic, peeled and finely chopped

2 fresh red chillies, deseeded and finely chopped

a 2cm piece of fresh ginger, peeled and finely chopped

4 Little Gem lettuces, quartered lengthways

400g fresh egg noodles

2 tbsp soy sauce

½ tbsp fish sauce

sesame oil, to drizzle

Heat half of the oil in a wok over a high heat. When hot, stir-fry the prawns for 2 minutes, until just cooked through. Place the cooked prawns on a plate and set aside.

Keeping the wok over a high heat, pour in the remaining tablespoon of oil. When hot, add the spring onions, garlic, chillies and ginger. Stir-fry for 1 minute and then add the lettuce. Gently mix together and fry for 2 minutes.

Return the prawns to the wok along with the noodles, soy sauce, fish sauce and a little sesame oil. Toss over a high heat until all of the ingredients are well mixed together and cooked through.

Forget about serving plates; whack the wok straight on the table and let everyone dig in.

'If food were a church,
then let me kneel and
pray until I'm full.'

ANGLO-ASIAN

Food without flavour is like a man without wit: useless and unnecessary.

I know I may be biased, but Asian cuisine is most definitely the best. Here is my argument: not only is Asian food tasty, it's also, more often than not, virtuously healthy and it's designed to share. And it's the sharing that I love the most; the art of giving and receiving with the people we care about. Huge bowls filled with gorgeousness, displayed at the centre of a round table for all to jump into.

I dedicate this chapter to Mama Wan who is the perfect combination of sweet and sour, who loves my Dad so much that she even adapted her cooking style to satisfy his tastes. So much so that our Sunday dinner always came with rice.

BEEF COBBLER WITH CORIANDER DUMPLINGS

505	CALORIES
18.4g	FAT
7.7g	SAT FAT
5.9g	SUGAR
2g	SALT

I consider myself to be very race lucky. Anglo-Asian means I've got the best of both worlds: an Asian culture steeped in history, amazing foods and traditions, and an English heritage bound by my love of this country. This next dish is truly a perfect representation of my 50/50 upbringing. Succulent beef, seasoned with five spices from the East, garnished with dumplings laced with deep and fragrant coriander. I dedicate this dish to my Mum and Dad: thank you for making East kiss West. Your love for one another will inspire my wok forever.

SERVES 6

1kg trimmed stewing steak, chopped into 2cm chunks (or use 1.25kg beef shin, meat removed and chopped into 2cm chunks)

3 tbsp rice bran oil or vegetable oil

1 red onion, peeled and diced

2 cloves of garlic, peeled and finely diced

2 sticks of celery, diced

2 star anise

a 6cm strip of orange zest

5 tomatoes, roughly chopped

100ml shaosing or dry sherry

25ml soy sauce

750ml hot reduced salt beef stock

white pepper

FOR THE CORIANDER DUMPLINGS

250g flour

40g butter, cut into cubes

2 tsp baking powder

3 tbsp chopped fresh coriander

3 tbsp chopped fresh chives

1 egg

125ml milk

Season the beef all over with a little pepper. Heat half the oil in a large flameproof casserole or ovenproof pan with a lid over a high heat until very hot. Fry the beef in batches for 2–3 minutes, until it is a rich deep brown colour all over. Remove the beef and keep to one side.

Wipe the pan with some kitchen roll, add the remaining oil and heat over a medium to high heat. Once the oil is hot, add the onion, garlic and celery and stir-fry for 3–4 minutes. Add the star anise and orange zest and continue to stir-fry for a further 2 minutes. Tip in the chopped tomatoes and the browned beef and cook for 2 minutes, until the tomatoes begin to break down.

Pour in the shaosing, soy sauce and hot stock, and bring the whole lot to the boil. Reduce the heat to a simmer, place a lid on top and cook for about 1½ hours, until the beef is tender.

While the beef is cooking, make the dumplings. Place the flour in a bowl and add the butter. Work the butter into the flour with your fingers until the mixture resembles breadcrumbs. Add the baking powder, coriander and chives, and mix together. Crack the egg into the mixture and pour in the milk. Using your hands or a wooden spoon, bring the whole mixture together to form a crumbly dough.

Preheat the oven to 190°C/375°F/Gas mark 5. Divide your dough into balls, each about the size of a golf ball (you should be able to get 6 or 7).

When the stew has finished cooking, drop in the dough balls; they should half-float on the surface. Replace the lid and cook in the preheated oven for 20 minutes, by which time the meat will be meltingly tender and the dumplings cooked through. Serve this hearty Asian-flavoured beef stew in bowls.

299
CALORIES
17.2g
FAT
6.2g
SAT FAT
4.3g
SUGAR
2.2g
SALT

STUFFED SPICED PUMPKIN WITH MINCED BEEF

This is a visual feast as well as an actual feast. You can make this using all sorts of vegetables: marrow, aubergine, even bell peppers. Just make sure you scoop out enough of the flesh so that the wall isn't too thick – it needs to be about 2–3cm otherwise it will take forever to cook. The cooking times will vary, but the flesh needs to be tender, while still holding its shape. Test it with a normal eating knife and it should slice fairly easily.

SERVES 4

2 tbsp rice bran oil or vegetable oil
500g lean minced beef
1 red onion, peeled and finely diced
2 fresh red chillies, deseeded and finely diced (leave in the seeds if you like it hot)
a 2cm piece of fresh ginger, peeled and finely diced
3 cloves of garlic, peeled and finely chopped
4 tinned anchovy fillets, drained and finely chopped
1½ tbsp Chinese five spice
1 tbsp oyster sauce
1 tbsp soy sauce
8 water chestnuts, drained and roughly chopped
1 x 1kg pumpkin
salt and white pepper

Heat half of the oil in a wok over a high heat. Once hot, add the beef and cook for 4–5 minutes, stirring occasionally, until browned all over. (You may need to do this in batches depending on the size of your wok.) Transfer the browned mince to a sieve placed over a bowl to drain off any excess fat.

Wipe out the wok with some kitchen roll and pour in the remaining oil. Heat over a medium to high heat and then add the onion and stir-fry for 3–4 minutes, until just softened. Add the chillies, ginger, garlic and anchovies and continue to stir-fry for 2 minutes, before adding the five spice and mixing well. Tip the mince back into the wok and add a splash of water along with the oyster sauce, soy sauce and the water chestnuts. Bring to the boil briefly before turning off the heat.

Preheat the oven to 180°C/350°F/Gas mark 5. Slice the top off the pumpkin and keep to one side. Use a spoon to scrape out all of the seeds to leave a generous cavity. The walls of the pumpkin should be about 2–3cm thick. Season the inside with salt and pepper, then spoon in the beef mixture. Replace the top on the pumpkin, place on a baking tray and roast in the oven for about 1 hour. By this time the flesh of the pumpkin should be tender to touch, but still firm enough to hold its shape. Place your cooked pumpkin on a serving plate and proudly place in the middle of the table as a beautiful edible centrepiece.

651 CALORIES
11.9g FAT
3.8g SAT FAT
7.7g SUGAR
2.1g SALT

SUGAR AND SALT PORK SHOULDER

A classic Chinese dish that you'll see hanging in the window of Chinese restaurants is roasted belly of pork, which is always served with a side dish of sugar. This is my take on that classic dish. It is guaranteed to have just as much flavour but is far healthier, and you don't need to trek to the nearest China Town to get it.

SERVES 8

3 tbsp sugar

2 tbsp salt

2kg boned pork shoulder

2 x quantities of steamed buns (see page 192)

1 iceberg lettuce, shredded

2 cucumbers, peeled, halved lengthways and deseeded, chopped into 1cm pieces

8 spring onions, trimmed and finely sliced

6 tbsp hoisin sauce

Mix together the sugar and salt and rub it into the pork, making sure to really work it into the meat. Leave in the fridge overnight.

About an hour before you want to cook the pork, remove it from the fridge and pat dry with kitchen roll. Preheat your oven to 220°C/425°F/Gas mark 7.

Place the pork on a wire rack arranged over an oven tray. Cook in the oven for 15 minutes, by which time the pork should have started to brown all over. Reduce the temperature to 150°C/300°F/Gas mark 2 and cook for a minimum of 1½ hours and up to 3 hours. After an hour of cooking, cover the pork with a layer of foil. The longer you cook the pork, the more succulent and tender it will become, until it starts to fall apart.

Remove the pork from the oven, wrap it in foil and leave to rest for 30 minutes.

When the half an hour is up, slice or shred the pork and serve it in the steamed buns, topped with lettuce, cucumber, spring onions and hoisin sauce for a roast dinner that nobody will forget.

599
CALORIES
31.5g
FAT
8.1g
SAT FAT
3.1g
SUGAR
2.2g
SALT

CHICKEN POT ROAST

For an Asian twist on your classic Sunday lunch, try this warming and slightly sweet alternative to a roast chicken. The ginger adds a subtle fiery heat and, instead of roast potatoes that will have you craving an afternoon nap, I'm serving it with chilli and anchovy broccoli for a splash of colour and a satisfying crunch.

SERVES 6

2 tbsp rice bran oil or vegetable oil

1 large chicken (about 1.5kg), string removed

5 spring onions, trimmed, halved and bashed

3 sticks of celery, roughly chopped, plus 5 tbsp chopped celery leaves, to serve

5 cloves of garlic, unpeeled, bashed

a 5cm piece of fresh ginger, peeled and chopped into large chunks

2 star anise

150ml shaosing or dry sherry

400ml hot chicken stock

white pepper

600g steamed jasmine rice, to serve

3 x quantities of red chilli and anchovy broccoli (see page 190), to serve

Preheat the oven to 180°C/350°F/Gas mark 4. Heat the oil in a large, flameproof casserole over a high heat. Season the chicken with a little pepper. When the oil is hot, place the chicken, breast side down, in the casserole. Turn the chicken every 1–2 minutes in the hot oil until it is golden brown all over. Transfer the chicken to a plate and lower the heat under the casserole to medium.

Stir-fry the spring onions, celery, garlic, ginger and star anise for 1 minute. Pour in the shaosing and hot stock. Place the chicken back in the casserole and bring to the boil. Clamp a lid on top and cook in the oven for 1 hour. Remove from the oven and leave the chicken to rest with the lid on for 15 minutes.

Serve the chicken with steamed rice and broccoli, and ladle over some of the cooking liquid. Scatter liberally with the chopped celery leaves.

DUCK AND WASABI COLESLAW BUNS

295
CALORIES

6.9g
FAT

1.7g
SAT FAT

9.5g
SUGAR

0.9g
SALT

I'm a self-confessed bun junkie. Little parcels stuffed full of goodies remind me of my childhood. Most Sundays you'd find my whole family packed into my auntie's restaurant, chowing down bun after bun. Asian buns are the equivalent of the English sandwich and this is my fiery take on everyone's favourite salad, coleslaw.

SERVES 4

4 skinless duck legs

6 tbsp hoisin sauce

2 heaped tbsp light mayonnaise

2 tsp wasabi

1 tsp rice wine vinegar

400g white cabbage, cored and finely shredded

2 fresh red chillies, deseeded and finely chopped (leave the seeds in if you prefer it hotter)

4 spring onions, trimmed and finely sliced

2 carrots, peeled and finely sliced into matchsticks

½ cucumber, peeled, deseeded and finely diced

1 x quantity of steamed buns (see page 192), to serve

Preheat the oven to 190°C/375°F/Gas mark 5. Cover the duck legs as thoroughly as possible with half of the hoisin sauce. Place the coated legs on a baking tray lined with baking paper and cook in the oven for 25 minutes, by which time they should have darkened slightly in colour and be completely cooked through. Remove from the oven and leave to cool to room temperature.

Meanwhile, mix together the mayonnaise, wasabi and vinegar. The mayonnaise should turn a satisfying light green colour. Place the shredded cabbage, chillies, spring onions and carrots in a bowl. Dollop on the fiery mayonnaise and mix until all of the vegetables are lightly coated.

Use your fingers or a couple of forks to pull the meat from the duck legs.

Fill the buns with duck, coleslaw, cucumber and the remaining hoisin sauce. It will get messy.

566 CALORIES
22.1g FAT
4.3g SAT FAT
6.2g SUGAR
2.2g SALT

TEMPURA FISH AND CHIPS

Quintessentially English, but virtuously Asian. Asia has been battering and frying fish for centuries, but in a slightly different way to how your local takeaway does it. Using carbonated water and cornflour produces a lighter, crispier consistency, and sweet potato chips are a healthier complementary carbohydrate. So, although this isn't entirely guilt free, the method of cooking means you can eat it far more smugly.

SERVES 4

150g cornflour
150g plain white flour, plus 2 tbsp
375ml sparkling water
vegetable oil, for deep-frying
4 x 150g skinless firm white fish fillets, such as cod, hake or coley, bones removed
2 tbsp light soy sauce
1 tbsp rice wine vinegar
salt and white pepper
100g watercress, to serve
1 x quantity of sweet potato chips (see page 189)

Mix the flours together in a bowl and whisk in enough of the sparkling water to make a batter with the consistency of single cream (you may not need all of the water).

Preheat the oven to 190°C/375°F/Gas mark 5. Pour the oil into a large heavy-based saucepan to a depth of about 10cm. Heat over a medium heat to 170°C (if you don't have a kitchen thermometer, test the temperature of the oil by dropping in a small cube of white bread; it should turn golden brown in about 12 seconds).

Season the 2 tablespoons of plain flour with salt and pepper. Dust each piece of fish with the seasoned flour and shake lightly to remove any excess. Coat the fish in the batter and then gently, and very carefully, lower two pieces into the hot oil. Fry the fish in two batches, so you don't overcrowd the pan, keeping the fish warm on a baking tray in the oven while you fry the second batch.

Mix together the soy sauce and vinegar to create a dipping sauce.

Serve the lightly battered fish alongside the sweet potato chips, soy dipping sauce and watercress for an Asian alternative to the most classic of English dishes.

Fortune cookie quote, circa 1986:

'Man who have hole in pocket, have smile on face until Friday.'

DESSERTS AND GOKTAILS

When I think of Asian desserts, toffee apples and bananas immediately spring to mind – overripe fruit, deep-fried and covered in molten sugar. This drives me mad because Asian desserts are far more sophisticated, elegant and well thought out than that.

Buns stuffed with cha sui pork, light custard tarts enveloped in flaky pastry, yellow bean pies and glutinous coconut jelly. Years and years have been invested into perfecting these cooking techniques.

Chinese desserts are actually often served before your main meal as a way of introducing the elements to come. This is probably the reason why they contain quite savoury flavours. They're also the only dishes in Asian cuisine that you order and eat on your own – no sharing here.

I've developed a handful of sweets and desserts and streamlined them for you, so you never have to subject yourself to a bowl of sticky mess again.

As far as I'm concerned, cocktails should be considered one of your five a day. I particularly love cocktails with interesting flavours – lemon grass, lychees, kumquats . . . and there's no difference between making a cocktail and preparing Asian food – it's all about respecting your own personal taste.

344
CALORIES
15.6g
FAT
7.9g
SAT FAT
25.2g
SUGAR
0.6g
SALT

COCONUT AND LYCHEE MUFFINS

OK, this may not strictly be a pudding, but these muffins are just too delicious to leave out. Lychees have a lightly perfumed flavour that is like nothing else on the planet, and, when twinned with the familiar flavour of coconut, will make you forget about boring old blueberry muffins forever. I've made them with oil instead of butter, which makes them healthier too.

MAKES 8 LARGE MUFFINS

250g self-raising flour

150g caster sugar

2 tsp baking powder

2 tsp freshly ground black pepper

90g desiccated coconut, plus a little extra, toasted, for decoration

170ml semi-skimmed milk

50ml sunflower oil

1 egg

150g tinned lychees

Preheat the oven to 180°C/350°F/Gas mark 4. Line an 8-cup muffin tin with muffin cases.

Tip the flour into a bowl and add the sugar, baking powder, pepper and coconut and stir to combine.

Pour the milk and oil into a jug, crack in the egg and whisk with a fork.

Drain the lychees through a sieve, but make sure you reserve the liquid. Place the lychees in a small food processor and blitz until smooth.

Pour the puréed lychees and the milk mixture into the dry ingredients. Use a wooden spoon to bring everything together to a smooth, thick batter.

Divide the mixture between the muffin cases. Cook in the oven for 25 minutes, until golden on top and a skewer inserted into the middle comes out clean. Place the tray on a wire rack and leave to cool for about 10 minutes.

Using a skewer, make about 10 small holes in the top of each muffin. Slowly pour about 2 tablespoons of the reserved lychee juice over each muffin, waiting a little between each spoonful for the sponge to drink in the sweet juice. Scatter over the toasted coconut.

Let the muffins cool fully in the tin before serving. They will keep for a couple of days in an airtight container in the fridge.

150
CALORIES
6.8g
FAT
2.8g
SAT FAT
5.9g
SUGAR
0g
SALT

PEANUT AND SESAME MOCHI

Asian food is often about texture as much as it is about flavour, and this dessert is an excellent example of the Asian love of a sticky, elastic consistency that we are not so familiar with in the West. It is so popular that, even though it originated in Japan, it can be found in almost every shop in every country across Asia. There are even fan clubs and ceremonies dedicated to the making and tasting of this surprising sweet. So, if you are feeling a little adventurous and want a genuine taste of The Orient then have a go at this recipe.

MAKES ABOUT 16

250g glutinous rice flour (from Chinese supermarkets)

65g caster sugar

5 tbsp desiccated coconut

80g raw peanuts, chopped

5 tbsp sesame seeds

2 tbsp icing sugar

cornflour, for dusting

2 tsp rice bran oil or vegetable oil

Place the flour, sugar and 300ml water in a bowl. Mix together with a spoon until well combined and the sugar has dissolved. Cover the bowl in cling film and cook in the microwave at maximum power (600w) for 4 minutes. (If you don't have a microwave, steam in a shallow bowl topped with a lid over a pan of boiling water for about 40 minutes.) Peel off the cling film and leave to stand until it is cool enough to handle.

Meanwhile, dry fry the coconut, peanuts, sesame seeds and icing sugar over a medium to high heat for about 5 minutes, stirring, until just starting to lightly brown. Tip on to a plate and leave to cool.

Once the mochi dough is cool enough to handle, tip it on to a clean surface dusted liberally with cornflour. Halve the dough and roll out one half to a rectangle about 30cm x 20cm. With the long side facing you, scatter over half of the toasted nut and seed mixture. Now lift the edge closest to you and begin rolling the dough over the filling, like a Swiss roll. Give the roll a little press all the way along so that it stays together.

Roll out a piece of cling film longer than the mochi, and spread half the oil evenly along its length. Place the mochi roll on the cling film and roll it up, tightly twisting together the ends like a Christmas cracker. Repeat the process with the remaining ingredients to make another mochi roll. Keep in a cool place for about an hour.

When ready to serve, unwrap the rolled mochi from the cling film, dust with a little extra cornflour and slice at 2cm intervals to create lots of little mouth-sized pieces of joy.

221
CALORIES
0.2g
FAT
0g
SAT FAT
57g
SUGAR
0g
SALT

MANGO AND LEMON GRASS SORBET

What could be more refreshing than a mango sorbet at the end of a summer's evening meal? I'll tell you what: a mango and lemon grass sorbet! The lemon grass ekes out a few more percentiles of delicious mango flavour. YUM.

SERVES 8

250ml water

4 stalks of lemon grass, outside husk removed, halved and bashed

zest of 3 limes

300g caster sugar

5 ripe mangoes, peeled and stoned

Pour the water into a saucepan and add the bashed lemon grass, lime zest and sugar. Bring the mixture to the boil, stirring a couple of times along the way, until all of the caster sugar has dissolved. Turn off the heat and leave the mixture to infuse for at least 2 hours.

Roughly dice the mangoes and place in a blender. Sieve the infused sugar syrup over the mango pieces and blitz the mixture to a purée. Discard the lemon grass and lime zest.

Pour the liquid into a container with a lid and freeze for a minimum of 6 hours, or preferably overnight.

Serve scoops of your refreshing sorbet with glasses of Champagne for a decadently delicious dessert.

118
CALORIES
0g
FAT
0g
SAT FAT
26.4g
SUGAR
0.1g
SALT

GREEN TEA AND CITRUS JELLY

This is a very beautiful and unusual way to enjoy one of Asia's finest ingredients; a method of turning what is normally a humble support act into the centrepiece of your dessert.

SERVES 6

10 sheets of gelatin

800ml green tea (made by infusing 4 green tea bags in hot water for 5 minutes)

150g caster sugar

2 tbsp lemon juice

FOR THE COCONUT CREAM
(optional)

200ml single cream

2 tbsp icing sugar

2 tbsp coconut cream

2 tbsp black sesame seeds

Place the gelatin in a bowl of cold water and leave to soften for about 5 minutes.

Pour the tea into a saucepan, add the sugar and place over a medium heat until the sugar has completely dissolved, stirring occasionally. Stir in the lemon juice and then remove from the heat.

Remove the gelatin leaves from the soaking water and gently squeeze to remove any excess liquid. Slowly lower the gelatin into the warm tea and whisk to dissolve. Leave to cool to room temperature.

Pour the jelly into your jelly mould(s) (either a single large mould or several smaller ones). Leave the jelly to set in the fridge for a minimum of 4 hours, or preferably overnight.

If you're making the coconut cream, whisk together the cream, icing sugar and coconut cream just before serving.

Remove the jelly from the fridge and, using one swift, smooth movement, tip it out on to your serving plate(s). If using, top the coconut cream with the sesame seeds and serve alongside the jelly.

SWEET CARDAMOM RICE

This dessert heralds from India and is a more interesting take on our classic rice pudding. Once you've tried the recipe a couple of times, don't be afraid to play around with other spices and flavourings like honey, cinnamon and even Chinese five spice.

359
CALORIES
9.3g
FAT
5.8g
SAT FAT
38.4g
SUGAR
0.3g
SALT

SERVES 6

1.5L semi-skimmed milk

5 cardamom pods, lightly bashed

1 vanilla pod, split lengthways and seeds scraped out

30g unsalted butter

150g pudding rice

80g caster sugar

500g fresh fruit, such as mangoes and pomegranate seeds, to serve

optional: pomegranate seeds and toasted nuts, to serve

Pour the milk into a saucepan and add the cardamom pods along with the scraped vanilla seeds and the vanilla pod. Bring the mixture slowly to the boil over a low heat and let it simmer for 1 minute. Turn off the heat and leave to infuse for about 30 minutes.

Melt the butter in a saucepan over a medium heat. Once bubbling, add the rice and stir to coat in the butter. Pour in the sugar and let it melt into the butter, stirring a couple of times. Strain the milk through a sieve into the rice and stir until well combined.

Let the mixture come to the boil and then reduce the heat and simmer for about 35 minutes, stirring frequently. The rice should be soft and the pudding should have a creamy consistency. You can eat it as it is, or pour it into an ovenproof dish (or individual ones) and grill for about 5 minutes, until crispy and caramelized on top.

230
CALORIES
2.4g
FAT
0.7g
SAT FAT
6.3g
SUGAR
0.9g
SALT

CHAR SIU BAO

Once you've finished flicking back through the last few pages, and assumed that the printer has made a mistake with the order of recipes, rest assured that this savoury dish is supposed to feature here in the dessert section. You see, in Asia, many people do not keep such rigid lines between their sweet and savoury courses. This surprisingly satisfying end to a meal will provide your guests with an authentic Asian experience.

MAKES 8

300g pork leg, chopped into 1cm pieces
¼ x quantity of Chinese barbecue sauce (see page 205)
1 x quantity of the steamed bun recipe (see page 192)
flour, to dust

Bring a large saucepan of water to the boil over a medium to high heat. Once boiling, drop in the chopped pork and cook for 1 minute. Drain through a colander and cool the meat by running it under cold water.

Pat the meat dry with some kitchen roll and place in a bowl. Pour over the barbecue sauce and mix well, ensuring all the meat is well coated.

Divide the dough for the steamed buns into 8 equal pieces. Roll out each piece on a floured surface to a round about 15cm in diameter and spoon an eighth of the meat into the middle of each round. Draw the sides up around the meat and squash the dough together at the top to seal. Twist the dough a little and trim away any excess. Carefully place the buns in your largest steamer basket (you may need to use two smaller steamer baskets).

Bring a wok of water to the boil and place the steamer basket on the top. Do not let the base of the basket touch the boiling water. Steam the buns for about 40 minutes, checking regularly that the water hasn't boiled away and topping up if necessary. Serve up your delicious dessert to astonished guests and revel in your Asian authenticity.

GOKTAILS

These recipes each serve one, but you can easily multiply the ingredients to make as many as you need.

FROZEN MANGO MARGARITA

50ml tequila
25ml mango liqueur
juice of ½ a lime
6 ice cubes
slice of mango, to garnish

Pour all ingredients into a blender with the ice. Blitz until smooth, then pour into a Margarita glass and garnish with a slice of mango.

RED LOTUS

50ml vodka
50ml lychee liqueur
200ml cranberry juice
4 ice cubes
lychees, to garnish

Pour all the ingredients into a cocktail shaker with the ice. Shake well and then strain into a tumbler or long glass. Add the ice and garnish with a couple of lychees on a cocktail stick.

ASIAN MIST

ice
dash of rum
50ml coconut rum (Malibu or similar)
25ml melon liqueur
lemonade
pineapple juice
slice of pineapple, to garnish

Fill a tall glass with ice and pour over the rum, coconut rum and melon liqueur. Mix together and then top up with equal parts lemonade and pineapple juice. Stir and then garnish with the slice of pineapple.

SAKE SUNRISE

120 CALORIES
0.1g FAT
0g SAT FAT
5.2g SUGAR
0g SALT

50ml Sake
50ml orange juice
a splash of Champagne
orange zest, to garnish

Shake the Sake and orange juice together with ice in a cocktail shaker and strain into a martini glass. Top up with Champagne, then garnish with orange zest.

GINGER MARTINI

183 CALORIES
0g FAT
0g SAT FAT
10.1g SUGAR
0g SALT

So, you really have to be prepared for this one! A week (or even longer, if possible) before your big night, buy a litre of vodka and drop in 50g shredded ginger. Leave in a cool dark place to infuse.

15ml sugar syrup
juice of ½ a lime
15ml Cointreau
50ml ginger-infused vodka
ice
lime zest, to garnish
sliver of fresh red chilli, to garnish

Mix the sugar syrup, lime juice, Cointreau and ginger vodka in a cocktail shaker with ice. Strain into a chilled tumbler filled with ice. Garnish with a little lime zest and a sliver of chilli.

'Cheers, McCullum, my pisshead partner, gossip confidante and pain in the arse.'

ASIAN MIST

ASIAN MARY

KUMQUAT MOJITO

IRISH PANDA

FROZEN MANGO MARGARITA

EASTERN PHIZZ

RED LOTUS

SAKE SURPRISE

RAFFLES HOTEL
SINGAPORE
"Stands for all the fables
of the exotic East..."
W. Somerset Maugham

GINGER MARTINI

IRISH PANDA

50ml soya milk
25ml Kahlua
50ml Bailey's
drizzle of honey
3 coffee beans
ice

Pour all ingredients into a cocktail shaker with some ice and shake well. Strain into a martini glass and garnish with the coffee beans.

ASIAN MARY

200ml tomato juice
50ml vodka
juice of ½ a lemon
a 1.5cm piece of fresh ginger, peeled and finely chopped
½ tsp wasabi
ice
dash of soy sauce
slice of fresh red chilli, to garnish
1 stalk of lemon grass, to garnish

Pour the tomato juice, vodka, lemon juice, ginger and wasabi into a cocktail shaker with ice. Shake well then pour over ice into a tall glass. Add a dash of soy sauce and stir until mixed. Garnish with the chilli and lemon grass. You can use as much or as little wasabi as you can handle!

KUMQUAT MOJITO

50ml dark rum
1–2 tsp sugar, to taste
10 fresh mint sprigs
1 kumquat or kalamansi, plus a slice of kumquat, to garnish
ice
200ml soda water

If you have time, leave the rum, sugar and mint leaves soaking for an hour or so before serving. Muddle all three together in the bottom of a tumbler and squeeze over the kumquat or kalamansi. Add ice and soda water and mix together. Garnish with a slice of kumquat for a truly south-Asian citrus flavour!

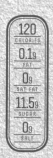

120
CALORIES
0.1g
FAT
0g
SAT FAT
11.5g
SUGAR
0g
SALT

EASTERN PHIZZ

25ml peach schnapps
25ml mango juice
ice
Champagne
optional: a thin slice of mango, to
    garnish

Pour the schnapps and mango juice into a
cocktail shaker with some ice and shake well.
Strain into a Champagne glass, top up with
fizz and give it a stir! For something a little
extra, garnish with a thin slice of mango.

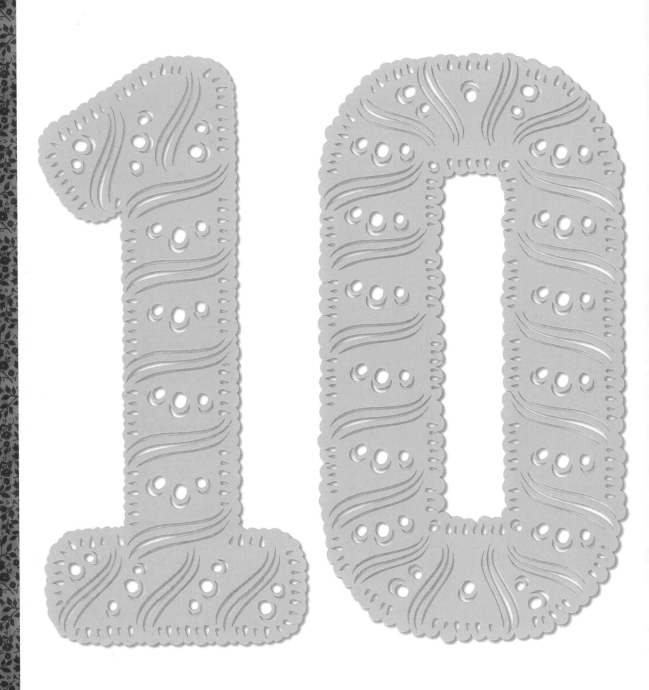

SIDES AND EXTRAS

For this chapter I'm going back to my day job. Think of your meal as your outfit; it needs balance and proportion and an injection of creativity. For the purpose of this exercise, the rice will be your little black dress: simple, elegant and a wardrobe staple. Your sauces will become your suiting: clean lines, sophisticated and as sharp as you'd like them. And all the sides and add-ons are the accessories that complete your finished look and elevate your style from everyday to out of this world.

What separates us from the animals is the ability to accessorize – a famous quote on which I've based most of my career. And the ability to accessorize can be the difference between happiness and sadness. A chiffon scarf or a pair of killer heels can fill you with woksful of confidence, and if you employ the same theory to your cooking, I can guarantee you culinary success.

At the Asian dinner table, the side dishes are just as important as the main events. It's all about respect. A simple pak choy tossed in sesame oil can steal the show against a roasted duck. The simple reason being that Asian food is designed to share, and there can sometimes be as many as 10 dishes on the table at any one time. If all of those dishes were packed with complex layers of flavour, then it could ruin the meal; the side dishes offer a moment's break, something simple to complement the main dishes. Think of them as the silent heroes.

120
CALORIES
5.5g
FAT
1.1g
SAT FAT
5g
SUGAR
0.4g
SALT

SWEET POTATO CHIPS

Everyone loves chips, but these are a healthier version made with sweet potato and they are baked rather than fried. They also add a vivid splash of bright orange to your plate – what more could you ask for?

SERVES 4

350g sweet potato, scrubbed clean, and chopped into 2cm chips
2 tbsp rice bran oil or vegetable oil
salt

Preheat your oven to 190°C/375°F/Gas mark 5. Arrange the chipped sweet potato on a baking tray lined with greaseproof paper. Drizzle over the oil and season with salt. Toss the potato pieces in the oil and salt so that they are all reasonably slicked.

Cook in the oven for about 45 minutes, turning a couple of times, until lightly golden and tender.

84
CALORIES
4.1g
FAT
0.8g
SAT FAT
2g
SUGAR
1.9g
SALT

RED CHILLI AND ANCHOVY BROCCOLI

Serve simply with plain rice for a deliciously frugal supper, or as a side dish for a larger, more substantial dinner.

SERVES 2 AS A SIDE DISH

250g broccoli

½ tsp rice bran oil or vegetable oil

1 clove of garlic, peeled and finely sliced

3 tinned anchovy fillets, drained and finely diced

1 fresh red chilli, deseeded and finely diced (leave in the seeds if you'd like it hotter)

1½ tbsp oyster sauce

Separate the broccoli florets from the stalk. Cut off and discard the woody bit from the base of the stalk. Slice the stalk in half lengthways before finely slicing into thin semi-circles. Pick through the florets, and if there are any that are much bigger than the others slice them in half or into quarters. You want the florets to be roughly the same size as each other.

When ready to cook, heat the oil in a wok over a medium to high heat. Once hot, add the sliced broccoli stalk and stir-fry for 1 minute before adding the florets. Add the garlic, anchovies and chilli and continue to stir-fry for a further 2 minutes.

Add 50ml of water; it should instantly steam up. Let it almost completely evaporate before pouring in the oyster sauce. Reduce the heat as low as it will go, and stir for a further minute so that the broccoli is completely coated in the sauce.

ขาวสูตร 1 ตราเด็กสมบู
หยั่นหว่อหยุ่น
政府註冊
肥兒商標
ตราเด็ก
สมบูรณ์
NAT
FER
ส่วนประกอบโดย
ประมาณ
น้ำ
ถั่วเหลือง 25%
แป้งสาลี
เกลือ
น้ำตาล
ใช้วัตถุปรุง
แต่งรสอาหาร
(ผงชูรส)
ใช้วัตถุกันเสีย
仁和醬園
300

158
CALORIES

0.6g
FAT

0.1g
SAT FAT

2.6g
SUGAR

0.2g
SALT

STEAMED BUNS

Although I've cooked with my steamer a million and one times, I never cease to wonder at the subtlety of the process that transforms raw ingredients to cooked, with very little noise or fuss. Fill these perfectly light buns with whatever takes your fancy.

MAKES 8

6g fast action yeast

175ml warm water

350g plain white flour, plus extra for dusting

15g sugar

1/3 tsp salt

Stir the yeast into the warm water until it has dissolved.

Place the flour, sugar and salt in a bowl and mix together. Add the warm yeasty water and begin mixing with a wooden spoon, until it becomes impossible and impractical.

Scrape the dough on to a lightly floured surface. Knead for about 5 minutes, until it is fully worked together and has formed a smooth dough. Shape the dough into a ball and place it in a bowl. Cover with cling film and leave in a warm place for about 2 hours, or until the dough has doubled in size.

Tip the dough back on to your floured surface and knead it lightly again to knock out the air. Divide the dough into 8 evenly sized balls. Place the dough balls in a steamer basket, leaving at least 5cm between each one. It is likely that you will have to use two steamer baskets, one on top of the other, or cook them in two batches. Leave the dough balls to rise in the steamer basket(s) somewhere warm for about 30 minutes, until doubled in size.

Pour water into your wok to a depth of about 10cm and bring to the boil over a medium to high heat. Place the steamer basket(s) on top (making sure the bottom of the basket doesn't touch the water) and steam the buns for 20 minutes, by which time they should have expanded and be fully cooked through. They should feel light to pick up. Keep an eye on the water levels in the wok, and top up as needed.

59
CALORIES

3.6g
FAT

0.7g
SAT FAT

1.9g
SUGAR

1.2g
SALT

BEAN SPROUTS IN OYSTER SAUCE

This clever little accessory can be added to almost any meal to add a little bit of extra flavour and crunchy texture.

SERVES 4

1 tbsp rice bran oil or vegetable oil

2 cloves of garlic, peeled and finely chopped

300g bean sprouts

1 tbsp oyster sauce

2 tsp light soy sauce

1 tsp fish sauce

1 tsp sesame oil

Heat the oil in a wok over a high heat. When hot, stir-fry the garlic for 30 seconds. Add the bean sprouts and continue to stir-fry for a further minute, then pour in about 2 tablespoons of water; it will steam and evaporate almost instantly.

Remove the wok from the heat and pour in the remaining ingredients. Mix together so that the bean sprouts are well coated in the sauce.

65
CALORIES
2.2g
FAT
0.3g
SAT FAT
8.8g
SUGAR
1.2g
SALT

VIETNAMESE SALAD

This recipe makes it in because it is so deliciously different to anything else that you may have tried. As soon as the sun shows itself, you should make this salad and serve it with any piece of grilled fish or meat; it is too good not to.

SERVES 4

1½ tbsp fish sauce

juice of 2 limes

2 tsp palm sugar or agave nectar

2 tsp sesame oil

2 fennel bulbs, trimmed and finely
   sliced

3 carrots, peeled and finely sliced

1 cucumber, peeled, halved lengthways
   and deseeded, finely sliced

3 tbsp fresh mint leaves

3 tbsp fresh coriander leaves

Pour the fish sauce and lime juice into a bowl. Add the sugar and sesame oil and mix together thoroughly until the sugar has completely dissolved.

Place the prepared vegetables and the herbs in a bowl and pour over the dressing. Toss together, and serve. Simple.

71
CALORIES
0.3g
FAT
0g
SAT FAT
0.3g
SUGAR
0g
SALT

DUMPLING DOUGH

The versatility of mixing flour and water together in different ratios never ceases to amaze me. Whether making flatbreads (see overleaf) or this dumpling dough, I will, at some point, find myself stopping to marvel at the beautifully basic process from which so many delicious things come. Use this recipe to make the skins for any of the dumpling recipes in this book.

MAKES ENOUGH FOR 12 DUMPLINGS

250g plain flour, plus extra to dust
125ml tepid water

Measure out the flour into a bowl. Pour in the water and mix together with your fingers. Once most of the water has been absorbed, tip the dough out on to a lightly floured surface.

Knead the dough for about 5 minutes, by which time the dough should have become fairly elastic and smooth. If it hasn't, then continue to knead for a couple more minutes. Once you are happy with the consistency, place the dough in a clean bowl, cover with cling film and leave to rest at room temperature for 30 minutes.

When you are ready to make the dumpling skins, halve the dough and roll each piece into a thick sausage shape. Divide each sausage into 6, so that you have 12 small pieces of dough. On a lightly floured surface roll out each piece until it is about 0.5cm thick and about 10cm in diameter.

Try to use your dumpling skins almost immediately as they will dry out quite quickly.

213
CALORIES

0.8g
FAT

0.1g
SAT FAT

0.9g
SUGAR

0g
SALT

FLATBREADS

Perfect for scooping, wrapping, dipping and using in place of a plate, flatbreads are endlessly versatile and very easy to make. Try to make them just before you need them, though, as they can dry out if prepared too far in advance.

MAKES 4 LARGE OR 8 SMALL
250g plain white flour, plus extra
   to dust
175ml water

Mix together the water and flour in a large bowl until you achieve a smooth dough consistency. Knead lightly and shape into a ball on a lightly floured surface, and place in a clean bowl. Cover with cling film and leave in a warm place for about 30 minutes.

KNEAD!!!

ROLL!!!

When ready to cook, divide the dough into evenly sized pieces. On a lightly floured surface, roll each piece into a round, about 0.5cm thick.

Heat a non-stick frying pan over a high heat.
When hot, dry-fry a flatbread for 2 minutes
on one side before flipping it over and
cooking for a further 2 minutes on the other
side. The flatbreads should be satisfyingly
brown in parts and lightly blistered. Repeat
with the remaining flatbreads.

274
CALORIES
0.5g
FAT
0.1g
SAT FAT
0.1g
SUGAR
0g
SALT

STEAMED RICE

Cooking rice often seems to throw people into a state of nervous panic, but follow my recipe and you will produce perfectly fluffy rice every time. This method works well for white rice, including jasmine rice. Brown rice can often take longer to cook and will absorb more water.

SERVES 4

300g rice (I like a mixture of
American long grain and jasmine)
450ml water

Place the rice in a bowl and cover with cold water. Let it soak for a minimum of 10 minutes, but no more than an hour. Drain the soaked rice through a sieve and run cold water over it until the water runs clear.

Tip the rice into a saucepan for which you have a tight fitting lid (the rice needs to come about a third of the way up the side of the pan). Pour in the 450ml water and place the pot over a high heat.

Once the water has come to the boil, place the lid on the saucepan and reduce the heat to the lowest setting. Leave the rice to cook like this for 12 minutes. DO NOT REMOVE THE LID, AND DO NOT STIR THE RICE. After 12 minutes, turn off the heat and leave the rice to sit on the hob with the lid on for a further 5 minutes.

Remove the lid and marvel at your perfectly cooked rice.

473
CALORIES

2.1g
FAT

0g
SAT FAT

5g
SUGAR

2.8g
SALT

SUSHI RICE

This is the sticky, seasoned rice that you will find wrapped up in seaweed on your plate of sushi. It does, however, have more uses than simply being a vehicle for raw fish; it is a deliciously different method of preparing rice to accompany most dishes.

SERVES 2

250g sushi rice
300ml water
2 tsp sugar
1 tsp salt
4 tbsp rice wine vinegar

Rinse the rice and tip it into a medium saucepan with a lid. Pour in the 300ml water and bring to the boil over a high heat. Once it has come to the boil, clamp on the lid, reduce the heat as low as it will go and leave to cook for 10 minutes. DO NOT REMOVE THE LID OR STIR THE RICE. After 10 minutes, turn the heat off and leave the rice to sit on the hob with the lid on for a further 5 minutes.

Only now should you remove the lid. Dissolve the sugar and salt in the vinegar and pour over the rice and mix through.

This type of rice is best eaten at room temperature. It does not store very well, so try to eat it in one sitting.

139
CALORIES

1.8g
FAT

0.3g
SAT FAT

19.8g
SUGAR

3.6g
SALT

CHINESE BARBECUE SAUCE

I've not yet found a meat that this sauce doesn't enhance. Whether it is barbecued pork belly or grilled chicken breast, this sauce seems to have the Midas touch in terms of flavour. Use it as a marinade or liberally coat pretty much anything and then roast, grill, griddle or fry. Feel free to adapt this recipe to your palate. If you like it hot, then add some chopped chillies, and if you like the sweet and sour vibe, then add some vinegar and up the sugar a little.

MAKES ABOUT 500ml (enough to
    coat meat for 6)

4 cloves of garlic, peeled and minced
    or grated

a 4cm piece of fresh ginger, peeled
    and minced or grated

250ml hoisin sauce

2 tbsp brown sugar

100ml shaosing or dry sherry

50ml soy sauce

1 tsp Chinese five spice

Place all the ingredients in a bowl and use a whisk to mix everything together thoroughly.

If using as a marinade, then try to leave the meat marinating overnight, or for a minimum of 2 hours.

6
CALORIES
0.1g
FAT
0g
SAT FAT
0.6g
SUGAR
0.3g
SALT

PICKLED GINGER

This is my version of the pink pickled ginger you find in a sushi box, but I find that this side goes well with even the most Western of treats, including cold hams and cheeses. It works well with almost anything that you think needs a bit of additional fire. It needs to be left to pickle overnight, so ensure that you start the process the day before you are planning to serve this side dish.

MAKES ABOUT 100g (10g/serving)

10 tbsp rice wine vinegar

5 tsp sugar

5 tsp salt

100g fresh ginger, peeled and sliced
  into thin strips

Pour the vinegar into a small bowl and add the sugar and salt. Give the mixture a good whisk, until all the sugar and salt granules have completely dissolved.

Add the slices of ginger to the pickling mix and stir to ensure that the ginger is well coated in the vinegar. Leave in the fridge overnight for the flavours to mingle. The pickled ginger will keep, covered in the fridge, for up to a week.

'Cook, eat, drink, laugh, smile, sleep. Not necessarily in that order, but must be done each and every day.' Gok X

昌興茶行有限公司
香港皇后大道西242-244號

INDEX

TSINGTA

BIERE · BEER · CERVE

青島啤酒

ACKNOWLEDGEMENTS

A huge thank you to everyone who has worked on this book.

Rob Allison, Laura Herring, David Eldridge, Sarah Lavelle,
Romas Foord, Sam Duffy, Laura Higginson, Hannah Robinson,
Sarah Bennie, Alex Cooper, Martin Higgins, Helen Arnold,
Carey Smith, Helen Everson, Jess Mills, John Junior, Raf Szybowski,
Carol Hayes, Mark McCullum, Sarah Nash, Trevor Leighton,
Charlie Duffy and Carrie Jones.

A special thank you to my friends and family who have all taught me
how to cook and, more importantly, eat.

And, of course, a massive thank you to all those who cook from this
book. Long may your taste buds ache with happiness.